INVITING JESUS INTO OUR *F*AMILIES

Will Bring Healing and Restoration in our African-American Families

BY

DR. LEONARD L. HOBBS

INVITING JESUS INTO OUR FAMILIES
Will Bring Healing and Restoration in our African-American Families
by Dr. Leonard L. Hobbs

Printed in the United States of America.

ISBN 9781498427371

Unless otherwise indicated, Scripture quotations are taken from the King
James Version (KJV) – public domain

www.xulonpress.com

DEDICATION

First and foremost, I give praise and honor to Jesus Christ, my Rock, and my Lord. Without the guidance and presence of the Holy Spirit, I would not have been able to complete this book. I would like to thank my wife Charlotte for standing beside me throughout my spiritual and educational journey in writing this book. She has been my inspiration and motivation for continuing to improve my spiritual relationship with Christ and to be about my Father's business. She is my soul mate, and I dedicate this book to her.

I also thank my wonderful children: Lynnardo, Tessa, Sharlee, and our beautiful grandchildren Cameron, Phoenix, Lynnard, and Zoey, for always making me smile and creating lasting family memories. I pray that one day they can read this book and understand the passion and love that I have for our family and race. I'd like to thank my parents Mr. Sylvester Hobbs and Mrs. Earlie Bea Hobbs for the love, support, and sacrifices they made for me to follow my ambitions throughout my childhood and adult life. Praise God for my siblings who I love and appreciate: Minnie, Wylie, Dolores, Annie, Lucy, Sylvester Jr., Sammie, James, and Cecil, who have always supported me throughout my career. I look forward to discussing this book with my family at future gatherings.

I would like to extend special thanks and appreciation to my church family — Elim Ministries of Orlando — especially my pastor, friend, and brother in Christ, Dr. Winfred Verreen. Without the spiritual food, prayers, encouragement, and mentoring, I would not have had the strength and perseverance to press through the challenges of writing this book.

A special thanks to my father in law Charles Phoenix and my mother in law Edith Phoenix who raised and educated a God fearing woman and blessed me with her for the rest of my life.

Finally, with all the distractions and temptations in this world, I praise God for giving me accountability partners, Pastor George Ellington, LTC (R) Kenneth Gambles, and Sister Betty Laster who kept me on track and accepted no excuses from me. Additionally, I would like to extend my deepest appreciation to my niece, Demetria Hobbs who served as my personal editor.

TABLE OF CONTENTS

LIST OF FIGURES

LIST OF TABLES

INTRODUCTION

T he healing and restoration of African-American families from a Biblical perspective is a subject that is close and personal to me. When I reflected on the path in which the African-American families are going, what I saw broke my heart and grieved my soul. I saw a broken-down structure of African-American families across the nation that is headed for destruction without a detour in sight. As an African-American, I have personally witnessed a once powerful, prideful, united and strong family foundation crumble right before my eyes in a very short time. I have seen broken homes, absent fathers, single parents, teen mothers, increases in divorces, decreases in marriages, acceptable co-habitation, excessive drug usage, black on black crimes, worldly lifestyles and dysfunctional families. These are powerful and negative observations that have created a broken thread in communities and homes. However, in the spirit, I can see things being turned around when we begin to stand on the Word of God. I believe God's Word is true in 2 Chronicles 7:14, "If my people, which are called by my name, shall humble themselves, and pray, and seek my face, and turn from their wicked ways; then will I hear from heaven, and will forgive their sin, and will heal their land."

Personally, I cannot help but ask myself a number of questions: What happened? What happened to the strong spiritual

African-American families of the past? Whatever happened to the fathers who refused to be separated from their families? Where are the priests, prophets, providers, and protectors in our African-American homes? In essence, where are the godly, responsible men who will take exception to calling women "my baby's mama"? What are they doing? These are some of the questions with potential answers that will be addressed in detail in this book. I know it will be impossible to provide all the answers. I know that many of the answers will be challenged and questioned, but I can start by providing some answers that have promise.

However, there are some things in life that will never change. People will be born, and people will die. Some people will love us, and others will hate us. There will always be disagreements among humankind. There will always be opportunities to love, and opportunities to forgive. However, my favorite is the Word of God. It will never change. Man does not have the power or the authority to change anything in God's Word. Regardless of what people in this world prefer to do or choose to do, the expectations and standards that God has for His people will always remain the same. The book of Revelations 22:18-19 says:

> For I testify unto every man that heareth the words of the prophecy of this book, If any man shall add unto these things, God shall add unto him the plagues that are written in this book: [19] And if any man shall take away from the words of the book of this prophecy, God shall take away his part out of the book of life, and out of the holy city, and from the things which are written in this book.

God is a God of order. He expects order in the home. Moreover, He also expects His church to line up with His Word. For there to be order in the family, we must first understand the family foundation and structure that God established from the beginning. It was "in the beginning" that God established a family structure that consisted of God first, man second, woman third, family fourth and then the church. Unfortunately, many people who go into the ministry rearrange God's order by placing their spouses and families last on the list, thereby sacrificing their relationship with them for the building of a church. There is nothing biblical or spiritual about that decision. It cannot be found in the Word of God.

Proverbs 30:11-12 says, "There is a generation that curseth their father, and doth not bless their mother. [12] There is a generation that are pure in their own eyes, and yet is not washed from their filthiness." My fear is that we are now living in such a generation with very few answers in sight. I am referring to young African-American boys and girls who have no respect for their fathers and do not honor their mothers. We have homes with young boys and girls who do not fear, love, or respect the fact that their parents are the adults. In fact, there are parents who live in constant fear of their children, legal authorities, and the government.

Nevertheless, from a young person's point of view, there is nothing wrong with what they are doing. I am talking about a generation that is not afraid of disrespecting its parents with words laced with profanity. This generation does not see anything wrong with wearing inappropriate clothing that is offensive to their parents. Today, it is not uncommon for a young girl to dress in clothing that reveals parts of her anatomy that are normally reserved for the unity of marriage. No! Clothing does not make a person, but it sends a strong message of whom and what you are following. However, in the eyes of young African-American brothers and sisters, there is nothing wrong with what they wear, what they listen to, what they do, where they go, whom they worship, or what they worship. On the other hand, before we as adults begin to judge young people critically, we need to take a closer look at ourselves.

What have we done or what have we not done to lead this generation to a place to be significant and successful?

Yes, I know some of these issues may seem insignificant and trivial. However, there is a lack of respect and honor being shown toward parents. Children today have little or no moral ethics, and very few role models that know the Word of God. Without spiritual role models, there will never be a strong foundation for young African-Americans to build upon for future success. For restoration and healing to take place in African-American families, we need to build a foundation that can withstand the storms of sin, cultural differences, economic crashes, and racial divides.

The methodology and research used for this book extends far beyond my opinion and experiences. It is a detailed look at the spiritual history of African-American families and their importance in the structure and foundation of the family. Answers to the various questions that will surface will be addressed from the use of countless reference books, Bibles, commentaries, internet sites, documentaries, personal interviews, and especially surveys on families, culture, religion, Christianity, the church, and African-American traditions.

From this study one shall see, from a spiritual point of view, how significant it is for an African-American man to be a priest, prophet, provider, and protector for his family. In addition, analysis and confirmation will be made on the loss of identity, vision, and purpose of young African-American boys and how it has affected the African-American family. All of this leads to a key point: the instrumental part and significance that an African-American man has in the home. Yes, many women have raised children who have done well and continue to flourish in society, but that is not the norm. In fact, those women are a minority. Their success should not be considered justification for African-American families in the future to be a single-parent homes headed by women. Please understand, I am not confessing to having a solution, but I do want to bring about awareness to a problem that is in desperate need of timely solutions.

I am only one of millions, but I am one willing to be used by God to make a difference in my race. I am one willing to influence future generations, and to speak life and hope into another brother or sister. If others were willing to do the same thing, African-Americans would see the power of unity through the addition of one plus one, with "each one reaching one" as reflected in Table 1, the power of one can easily change an entire generation.

TABLE 1 THE POWER OF ONE

The Power of One	The Results of One
1+1	2
2+2	4
4+4	8
8+8	16
16+16	32
32+32	64
64+64	128
128+128	256
256+256	512
512+512	1,024
1,024+1,024	2,048
2,048+2,048	4,096
4,096+4,096	8,192
8,192+8,192	16,384
16,384+16,384	32,768
32,768+32,768	65,536
65,536+65,536	131,072
131,072+131,072	262,144
262,144+262,144	524,288
524,288+524,288	1,048,576

1. GOD'S FOUNDATION FOR A FAMILY

Anything not built on a solid foundation will not stand. When storms and adversity come, and they will come, the foundation will crumble. Unfortunately, in these days and times, African-American family foundations are weak. Instead of being built with the hands of God, its foundation has been laid by man. Nothing built upon the foundation laid by the hands of man will have the strength to withstand the storms of life and thus can easily be destroyed.

Luke 6:47-49
Whosoever cometh to me, and heareth my sayings, and doeth them, I will shew you to whom he is like [48] He is like a man which built an house, and digged deep, and laid the foundation on a rock: and when the flood arose, the stream beat vehemently upon that house, and could not shake it: for it was founded upon a rock. [49] But he that heareth, and doeth not, is like a man that without a foundation built an house upon the earth; against which the stream did beat vehemently, and immediately it fell; and the ruin of that house was great.

As African-Americans, we find ourselves today living upon a foundation that has been shaped by today's culture, a culture that is trying to take God out of everything that interferes with its conscience or threatens its worldly pleasures. However, it is impossible to establish a relationship with a God we do not know. Moreover, if we do not know Him, how can we possibly fear and obey Him? To understand God and establish a solid foundation for a family, we cannot fail to assemble ourselves in the House of God or position ourselves to hear the voice of God.

Nevertheless, it is a disturbingly, well-known fact that African-American women outnumber African-American men in the church. However, what is not known and continues to be a major problem in the African-American community is why so many African-American men are absent from church during Sunday morning services. These are men whose wives, daughters, and sons leave the home on Sunday to worship God and to be spiritually fed while the head of their household is at home. These are men who have fathered children, but are failing to take the time to be fathers. They are men who have no spiritual or godly roles in the lives of their children. It makes one wonder why there are not more fathers and Christian men in the house of God for Sunday morning service.

African-American men see religion as being for women: too passive, too soft, and too emotional. Drawing from his own surveys, the writer Kunjufu offers additional reasons for the poor showing of men at church: not wanting to dress up; not wanting to give their household authority over to the pastor and, for many, the heavy influence of Sunday sports in their lives. [1]

---

[1] Gina Steep. Are Men Anti-Church. Retrieved March 5, 2011 from http://www.vision.org/visionmedia/article.aspx?id=141

Excuses for men not attending church are numerous. Some of the excuses that men have given for not attending church are: 1) the dishonesty of the men in the pulpit and in leadership roles in the church, 2) failure to preach on issues that are important to men, 3) public failures of clergy, 4) sermons that do not personally speak to them, 5) communication style of clergy, 6) not meeting people where they are, 7) lack of respect for fathers, 8) poor examples of men from their home and families, 9) not believing church attendance is necessary for salvation, and 10) other priorities.

In fact, one of the strongest reasons men gave for refusing to attend church is the lack of masculinity from the teaching of the gospel and Christian beliefs. Men look at Christianity as a watered down, weak gospel that caters to women and children.

Islam apparently understands these masculine needs and purportedly is one of the fastest-growing religions in the world, especially among males, particularly black males. To understand why this might be the case, we return to Kunjufu's surveys.

He reports that his black male parishioners consider the church to be a place for passive wimps and other weak people who need help. He cites the following responses as general: "Men are conquerors and protectors and are supposed to protect their turf;" "I don't turn the other cheek, and I don't teach my sons to turn the other cheek; can you imagine, with all the violence going on in the community, me telling my son to, 'suck it up'?" Author, Dr. Leon Podles muses that, "Because they were for so long humiliated by whites, perhaps it's even more important for black males to be masculine."

In fact, there are two distinct strains of Islam: one sees Jihad as a spiritual battle against the evil within individuals, while the other sees it as a physical, literal battle against unbelievers. However, despite its differences, they both share one common theme: each one has a stronger masculine message than today's Christianity and, as a result, it has a more solid male presence to show for it. On the other hand, it is interesting to note that the same can be said of Judaism. Podles points out, "The majority of the practitioners of Judaism in America are men." [2]

What are the messages in modern Christianity that suggest feminine themes? Podles notes that women tend to "avoid conflict," and have "greater awareness of and loquacity about emotions." He says, "The religion of the heart flourished in both Protestantism and Catholicism, and the heart has been a feminine one." Over time,

>...as the Church became more and more feminized, the predominance of feminine emotions encouraged a subtle change in Christianity to make it conform more to the desires of the feminine heart. A change of emphasis here, a neglect of inconvenient Scripture there, and soon a religion takes a shape that, though difficult to distinguish from the Christianity of the Gospels, somehow has a quite different effect.

Indeed, the struggle for inner change and eradicating error has all but disappeared from modern Christianity, in favor of a message of universal acceptance that does not require self-mastery. [3]

Kunjufu's surveys show that men consider the church to be "emotional." Podles is not surprised. "For a man to talk freely and at length about his emotions sounds feminine; what seems to have happened is that women (in part) constructed an image of Jesus as they wished men were: sensitive, willing

---

[2] Gina Steep. Are Men Anti-Church. Retrieved March 5, 2011 from http://www.vision.org/visionmedia/article.aspx?id=141

[3] Gina Steep. Are Men Anti-Church. Retrieved March 5, 2011 from http://www.vision.org/visionmedia/article.aspx?id=141

to show themselves in speech, always ready to talk about their relationship. Podles says that men do not object to a message of love, but they object to the revelation of that love through words rather than actions.

The revelation of love may not be something men could or should change. Surely, the demonstration of one's convictions carries more weight than a description of them. Podles insists that men are looking for a way to "escape the shallowness and realize the seriousness of life," and that Christianity could be the means to channel the more destructive and violent energies of masculinity into a masculine model of self-mastery and self-control. "Carrying forward the traditions of the Jewish people, the Church converts the sort of 'unruly male' into the father of the family, and that's not an easy thing to do."[4]

Podles believes that even if men are attracted and return to church, he says, "They will not stay long in a feminized church. The Church must develop the best understanding of the meanings of masculinity and femininity, understanding that is consistent with human realities and the data of Scripture, only then will men return to the Church."[5]

In other words, "the church" needs to be prepared when men show up for church: prepared to meet their spiritual needs, prepared to get them involved, and prepared to listen and respond. Most of all, the church must be prepared to make changes for the good of the Body of Christ.

It is interesting to note that the black community in America was born in the absence of religious freedom. First there was the concerted, though not completely successful, effort to destroy the African religious traditions that the slaves tried to preserve. Then there were the prohibitions,

---

[4] Gina Steep. Are Men Anti-Church. Retrieved March 5, 2011 from http://www.vision.org/visionmedia/article.aspx?id=141

[5] Ibid.

which were adopted across the South, on preaching even the Christian gospel to slaves. However, negative prescriptions did not prevent blacks from grasping the power of the biblical message.[6]

Today's church has developed a culture that is driving men away. Almost every man in America has tried church, but two-thirds find it undeserving of a few hours for one day per week. When men need spiritual sustenance, they go to the wilderness, the workplace, the garage, or the corner bar. They watch their heroes in the stadium or on the racetrack. They plunge into a novel or sneak off to a movie. Church is one of the last places men look for God. More than 90 percent of American men believe in God, and five out of six call themselves Christians. Only two out of six attend church on a given Sunday. The average man accepts the reality of Jesus Christ, but fails to see any value in going to church.[7]

The truth is that most men in the pews grew up in church. Many of these lifers come not because they desire to be transformed by Christ, but because they enjoy participating in comforting rituals that have changed little since their childhood. There are also millions of men who attend a church service under duress, dragged by their mothers, wives, or girlfriends. What a contrast this is to the men of the Bible. Think of Moses and Elijah, David and Daniel, Peter and Paul. They were lions, not lambs; take-charge kind of men who risked everything in service to God. They fought valiantly and spilled blood. They spoke their minds and stepped on the toes of religious people. They were true leaders, tough people who were feared and respected by their community. All of these men had two things in common: 1) They had an

---

6 Dwight N. Hopkins. Black Faith and Public Talk. (Maryknoll, New York:Orbis Books; 1999), 20.

7 Dwight N. Hopkins. Black Faith and Public Talk. (Maryknoll, New York:Orbis Books; 1999), 20.

intense commitment to God and 2) they were not what you would call saintly.

In today's society, the men who regularly attend church service fall into two categories: 1) they are under 14 years old or 2) they are over the age of 60. Boys come because their mothers make them attend, and older men often establish church membership when their health begins to fail. Adult men in their twenties, thirties, and forties that are active in black churches also tend to be involved in a variety of other activities in the community and, as a result, are often over-committed. In addition, their congregations often rely heavily on these men, who are relatively few, for volunteer activities within the church and in the surrounding community, leaving them little time for other volunteer tasks. As a result, adult women, particularly those over forty, form the backbone of many churches, in addition to assuming leadership roles over Christian education, Bible studies, youth ministries, prayer meetings, music ministry, and praise and worship services. That explains why men feel left out and uncomfortable in the church.

Fathers need to raise their children in Christ. The phrase "in the discipline and instruction of the Lord" refers to the quality of training in the home. Quality training is what ensures quality control. Discipline and admonition that are not "of the Lord" can quickly degenerate to verbal or physical abuse. That kind of behavior does not meet the standards of Christ.[8]

When a father disciplines and instructs his children in the admonition of the Lord, he is under the quality control of the Holy Spirit. His primary purpose is to train a child, not abuse the child. The fact that he is under the influence of this quality control, rather than out of control is, in and of itself,

---

[8] Steve Farrar. Point Man. How A Man Can Lead His Family. (Frisco, Texas: Multnomah Books; 2003), 198.

an example to his children of the way they are to handle their children when they become parents. This quality control is to be modeled so that it can be imitated by the next generation.[9]

However, this assumes that there are active fathers in the home. That is not the case in a typical African-American home. What is typical is a missing father, missing in action from home and the church, while single mothers wait for fathers to grow up. The Bible warns us about this kind of immaturity in 1 Corinthians 13:11, "When I was a child, I spake as a child, I understood as a child, I thought as a child: but when I became a man, I put away childish things." As a result, single parents are left praying the scriptures in Philippians 4:6-7, "Be careful for nothing; but in everything by prayer and supplication with thanksgiving let your requests be made known unto God. [7] And the peace of God, which passeth all understanding, shall keep your hearts and minds through Christ Jesus." They are hoping and searching for help and peace from the Lord.

✶Man was created to dwell in the presence of God. Birds were created to soar with wings and fly. Unlike the birds, men are lost and do not know they need God's presence. The hunger and thirst for Him will lead us to give up the cherished masculinity and worship the true and loving God. For in Him we live, and move, and have our being.✶

Acts 17:26-28
And hath made of one blood all nations of men for to dwell on all the face of the earth, and hath determined the times before appointed, and the bounds of their habitation; [27] That they should seek the Lord, if haply they might feel after him, and find him, though he be not far from every one of us: [28] For in him we live, and move, and have our being; as certain

---

[9] Ibid.

also of your own poets have said, For we are also his
offspring.

If we are going to rehabilitate the hurting men around us,
we must teach them to worship. We must help them find the
secret place in the presence of God and recline there. Worship
is not effeminate. Neither is it for wimps. It is for giant killers
like David! It is for men of war like Samson! Give men His
presence, and they can withstand Delilah. Give them His
presence before they lose their battles with lust. [10]
The presence of God is a healing balm for men whose
stress cannot be resolved in a bottle of Scotch. His presence
brings hope to ex-junkies who desperately need to fill their
lives with God and overcome the addictive habits embedded
in their souls, lest the enemy come back and find an old house
cleaned, but empty![11]
If we can get men in God's presence to experience His
Glory and power, the Holy Spirit will touch every sinful
thought and part of their being. The challenge is getting men
into God's house and keeping them busy for the Lord.
So what is a man to do who burns with a desire to con-
tribute something to the life of the church? He can become a
minister, a deacon, or a trustee; these are three of his limited
options. However, most men want to participate in the daily
functioning and operation of the church. Nevertheless, when
we look at the makeup of the church, the only man who has a
leadership position in the church is the pastor, leaving the few
men who are in the church to sit, listen, and wait to go home
to assume a role in which they feel needed and appreciated.
Young African-American men and boys need to see
African-American men who are not pastors in leadership.

[10] Steve Farrar. Point Man. How A Man Can Lead His Family. (Frisco,
Texas: Multnomah Books; 2003), 198.

[11] Ibid.

Young men and boys need to see responsible men who love the Lord and are willing to take their proper roles in the church and the home. The problem that we have in the church is that the majority of African-American pastors are intimidated and threatened by other gifted, talented, and educated black men in the church. It is important for men to know that what they do matters to them, and to others as well. Men want to touch hearts and be difference-makers. They cannot do that by merely sitting in the church pews. Men like to use their hands and minds to build and create. Men want to be in positions that will allow them to meet needs and feel productive. Young men will only begin to understand and mirror the behavior of their fathers when their fathers invest time with them by doing things together. Time will create a bond and a foundation that cannot be broken; a bond that will leave memories well beyond their adolescent years. It is the kind of foundation that lasting and productive relationships and memories are built upon that will last a lifetime. It will serve as a blueprint for future generations.

2. THE ABSENT FATHER

When the scripturally undesirable becomes the acceptable in society — in other words, when sin becomes the norm — red flags should go up in churches and homes, warning us that it is time to preach and live the truth of God's Word. The absence of fathers in the home is scripturally unacceptable. Unfortunately, due to the decay of moral and religious standards in society today, the lack of fathers in the homes of their children is steadily increasing to the point where the presence of a father in the home is fast becoming a historic event. This declining presence has had and continues to have negative effects on children's relationships in the home, school, neighborhood, and society.

As Christians, we are taught to uphold the truth, regardless of society's desire to do things that are pleasing to its flesh. The book of Isaiah 59:14 says, "And judgment is turned away backward, and justice standeth afar off: for truth is fallen in the street, and equity cannot enter." We should never sit in the comfort of our homes and churches doing nothing about the sins and lies that are shoved in our faces. When we choose to get up, get out, and do something, the truth will stand.

The statistics on absent fathers in Table 2 are alarming. They represent some major challenges young African-Americans face; those who find themselves growing up in homes without their fathers.

TABLE 2 STATISTICS ON FATHERLESS CHILDREN IN AMERICA[12]

Challenges	Statistics
Incarceration Rates	Young men who grow up in homes without fathers are twice as likely to end up in jail as those who come from traditional two-parent families...those boys whose fathers were absent from the household had double the odds of being incarcerated even when other factors such as race, income, parent education and urban residence were held constant.
Suicide	63% of youth suicides are from fatherless homes.
Behavioral Disorders	85% of all children that exhibit behavioral disorders come from fatherless homes.
High School Dropouts	71% of all high school dropouts come from fatherless homes.
Educational Attainment	Kids living in single-parent homes or step-families report lower educational expectations on the part of their parents, less parental monitoring of school work, and less overall social supervision than children from intact families.
Juvenile Detention Rates	70% of juveniles in state-operated institutions come from fatherless homes.
Confused Identities	Boys who grow up in father-absent homes are more likely than those in father-present homes to have trouble establishing appropriate sex roles and gender identity.
Aggression	In a longitudinal study of 1,197 fourth-grade students, researchers observed "greater levels of aggression" in boys from mother-only households than from boys in mother-father households.

---

[12] http://fatherhood.about.com/od/fathersrights/a/fatherless_children.htm

Challenges	Statistics
Achievement	Children from low-income, two-parent families outperform students from high-income, single-parent homes. Almost twice as many high achievers come from two-parent homes as from one-parent homes.
Delinquency	Only 13 percent of juvenile delinquents come from families in which the biological mother and father are married to each other. By contrast, 33 percent have parents who are either divorced or separated and 44 percent have parents who were never married.
Criminal Activity	The likelihood that a young male will engage in criminal activity doubles if he is raised without a father and triples if he lives in a neighborhood with a high concentration of single-parent families.

The numerous challenges faced by African-American families are a major concern. We have a good reason to take a closer look at the bigger picture; the one that goes beyond what we want and what makes us feel good to what is best for a young generation that is lost without fathers investing in their lives.

It should never be an option for a father to invest in the lives of his children. It is not optional in the sight of God. God requires man to line up in the order He has ordained. Figure 1, "God's Order of Responsibility" and 1 Corinthians explains how we should line up as a family from a scriptural perspective. 1 Corinthians 11:3, "But I would have you know, that the head of every man is Christ; and the head of the woman is the man, and the head of Christ is God."

29

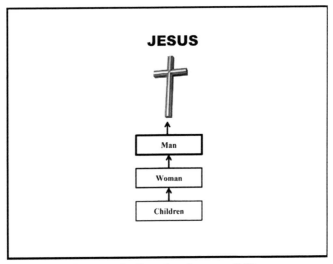

Figure 1. God's order of responsibility.

However, society's view of family responsibilities is now viewed by this generation with the role and position of man completely vacant as shown in Figure 2, "Society's Order of Responsibility." Yes, women can do numerous things without men. However, the role of real men of God should never be overlooked or downplayed because of an absent father and the opinions of a lost and sinful world that has forgotten the Creator.

When we look at a family from a triangular view, the father is shown as the foundation on which the family is built. Without a father, the foundation is lost and subject to fall.

Successful maturity of a man requires him to identify with both his mother and father. At some point in his life, the mother-son triangle must be replaced with the father-mother-son triangle. The lack of a father results in no transfer of identification from the mother to the father and the son remains imprisoned in his identification with the mother. The father's absence automatically increases the influence of the mother, who is consequently loaded with a duty that will become too heavy for her to bear. In these circumstances, the triangle

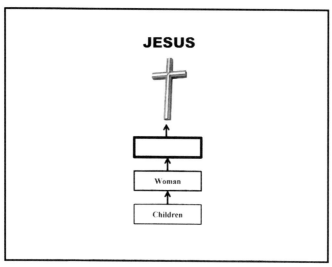

Figure 2. Society's order of responsibility.

never gets a chance to form properly; the immediate result is that, with regard to their sexual identity; sons develop into giants with feet of clay.[13]

In the construction field, clay would not be the best choice for the foundation and would not stand up to the test of time. On the other hand, cement is a solid material for the foundation, and that is what a father is to a family. When the father is in place, as represented in Figure 3, "Father-Son-Mother Triangle," the thought or idea of a father leaving the home is not a fear for his family. When fathers are present, his children are given the opportunity to be raised in an environment where they may mature and develop.

On the other hand, when the father's presence is not in the home, the family triangle is flipped upside down as shown in Figure 4, "Upside Down Family Triangle." The upside down triangle shows the position of the mother on top of a

---

[13] Guy Corneau, Absent Fathers, Lost Sons. The Search for Masculine Identity. (Boston, Massachusetts: Shambhala Publications, Inc; 1991), 16.

family that has been turned upside down, facing the wrong direction with a significant missing part — the father. Just because a family can function in this condition does not make it an acceptable choice in the eyes of God.

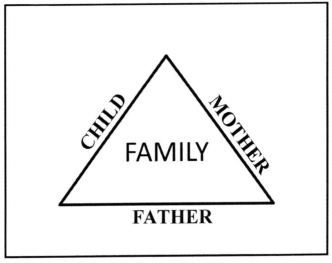

Figure 3. Father-son-mother triangle.

There have been too many circumstances where the mother's anger and/or vindictiveness towards the father of her child/children has led to an estranged relationship between father and child. A child should never be denied the opportunity of having a relationship with his or her father. It is time for parents to grow up and be parents, and put aside their differences for the sake of the child.

(¶) The roles of prophet, priest, protector, and provider in the family are designed for a father and should be fulfilled by a father and not a mother as depicted in Figure 5. In fact, the mother or wife should look to the father or husband to stand by her side and lead the family. When the mother or wife looks to the father or husband, she is honoring God's divine order for

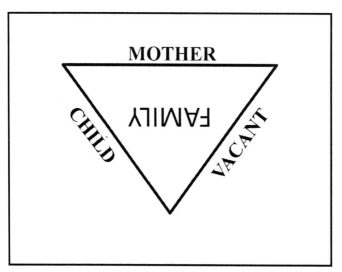

Figure 4. Upside down family triangle.

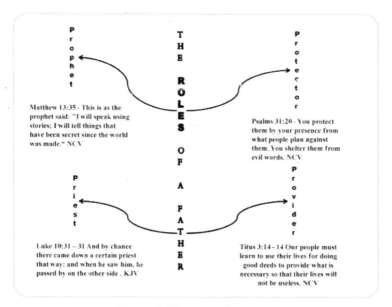

Figure 5. The roles of a father.

the structure of the family. She is also allowing the children an opportunity to see and experience the attributes of real men. To a man, being the head of the family implies leadership. As the head, men are expected to be leaders of the home. The Word of God supports this in Ephesians 5:23, "For the husband is the head of the wife, even as Christ is the head of the church: and he is the Saviour of the body."

The expectations for men are to lead their wives and children as Christ leads them. A man should lead by being the prophet of the home, positioning himself to hear the Word from God for the family. He should be the priest of the family, delivering the Word of God in his home. He should be a protector, always assuring his children and family that he is there to protect them, and there is nothing for them to fear. As the man and leader of the family, it should be a known fact that if anything is needed, he is the provider of his home; not any government-assisted programs, not relatives, not the church, but he is called to be the provider.

As our society continues to get farther and farther away from God, so have the hearts of fathers from their children and the hearts of children from their fathers. The scriptures warn us in Malachi 4:5-6, "Behold, I will send you Elijah the prophet before the coming of the great and dreadful day of the LORD: [6] And he shall turn the heart of the fathers to the children, and the heart of the children to their fathers, lest I come and smite the earth with a curse." There is double emphasis applied to the turning of hearts for fathers and children, when we see it stated again in the book of Luke. We should know that it is important to the Lord that our hearts are turned in the right direction as written in the book of Luke.

Luke 1:12-17
And when Zacharias saw him, he was troubled, and fear fell upon him. [13] But the angel said unto him, Fear not, Zacharias: for thy prayer is heard; and thy

wife Elisabeth shall bear thee a son, and thou shalt call his name John. |14| And thou shalt have joy and gladness; and many shall rejoice at his birth. |15| For he shall be great in the sight of the Lord, and shall drink neither wine nor strong drink; and he shall be filled with the Holy Ghost, even from his mother's womb. |16| And many of the children of Israel shall he turn to the Lord their God. |17| And he shall go before him in the spirit and power of Elias, to turn the hearts of the fathers to the children, and the disobedient to the wisdom of the just; to make ready a people prepared for the Lord.

We have become too familiar and comfortable with our relationships with God. We have put Him in a box and set boundaries for Him that we can understand. God is too big and mighty for anyone to contain Him in thought or deed. He is a God of mercy and grace, but He is also a God of righteousness, a God of Holiness, and a God who expects obedience from His children. The last thing anyone should want is for God to punish the children for their parents' actions. So we should not take Numbers 14:18 lightly, "The Lord is longsuffering, and of great mercy, forgiving iniquity and transgression, and by no means clearing the guilty, visiting the iniquity of the fathers upon the children unto the third and fourth generation." As African-Americans, we have had more than our share of adversity and should make it a priority to do the right thing to set our families up to be blessed and not cursed.

We need to be mindful of the things we do and the things we put before God because we serve a jealous God. Deuteronomy 5:9, "Thou shalt not bow down thyself unto them, nor serve them: for I the Lord thy God am a jealous God, visiting the iniquity of the fathers upon the children unto the third and fourth generation of them that hate me." Our young generation has enough in society to deal with, without having to deal with the sins of fathers.

The term "absent fathers" refers to both the emotional and the physical absence of fathers and suggests both spiritual and emotional absence. It also suggests the notion of fathers who, though physically present, behave in ways that are unacceptable: authoritarian fathers, for example, are oppressive and jealous of their sons' talents and smother their sons' attempts at creativity or self-affirmation.[14]

An individual's emotional identity is based on his sense of the spine that provides him with support from the inside. The father's absence results in the child's lack of an internal structure; this is the very essence of the negative father complex. An individual with a negative father complex does not feel structured. His ideas are confused; he has trouble setting goals, making decisions, deciding what is good for him and identifying his needs. For him, everything is mixed up; love and reason, sexual appetites and the simple need for affection. He sometimes has problems concentrating; all sorts of insignificant details distract him, and in severe cases, he has difficulty organizing his perceptions. He never feels sure about anything.[15]

The distinguishing feature of this negative father complex is an internal disorder that can range from a slight sense of confusion to severe mental disorganization. Men who are faced with a negative father complex will attempt to compensate for it by structuring them from the outside. This external structuring, however, will take on different accents, depending on whether a person is a Mr. Nice Guy, an obnoxious drunk or some other type.[16]

---

[14] Guy Corneau, *Absent Fathers, Lost Sons. The Search for Masculine Identity.* (Boston, Massachusetts: Shambhala Publications, Inc; 1991), 13.

[15] Guy Corneau, *Absent Fathers, Lost Sons. The Search for Masculine Identity.* (Boston, Massachusetts: Shambhala Publications, Inc; 1991), 37.

[16] Ibid. 37.

The more fragile a man feels internally, the more likely he is to try to build an outer shell to hide this fragility. This shell may take the form of bulging muscles or a bulging belly. Similarly, the more categorical, direct, and outspoken a man's opinions are, the more they mask a basic lack of certainty. Rebellious sons try to structure themselves by joining gangs that are essentially fascist; they give obedience to a primitive father. Eternal adolescents, they are looking for spiritual masters despite their apparent anarchy.[17]

In other words, because of the absence of so many African-American fathers in today's society, we have minimized the importance of a father in our lives and the lives of our children. The absence of a father is now accepted as the norm in households today. The devil has fed us a bucket of lies, to the point that we have not only accepted his lies, but we fight to enforce them. Then we get angry with anyone who disagrees with our beliefs and position on our sinful decisions.

We say we want to be free, but we want to be free on our terms. We do not want to hear the truth and when we do hear it, we reject it, because it conflicts with what we want. It challenges us to do right, and it convicts us of our sinful decisions. Yes, the truth does what the truth is supposed to do; it convicts our souls.

The truth is African-American fathers are extremely important and instrumental in the spiritual, emotional, and physical development of young children. Without the right foundation, our young black kids do not have a solid base of truth to build upon for the future.

During our lifetime, we will have the privilege of establishing a relationship with three fathers: 1) Our biological father, 2) our spiritual father (Satan), the father of lies, and 3) our Heavenly Father, the King of Kings, Lord of Lords, Jesus Christ, the third and final Father.

---

[17] Ibid, 38.

We have no input into whom our biological fathers are. At birth they are who they are, good or bad, absent or present; they are our biological fathers for life. Our first spiritual father we serve, believe it or not, is Satan. We can acknowledge his presence and power early in our lives, shortly after telling our first lie. When we sin and choose not to walk in obedience to the Word of God, we are doing what our father wants. When we cause confusion and division, we are doing what our father wants. When we rob, kill, and destroy others, we are doing what our father wants. We do it without questioning him. Do you get the picture? Satan is the father of sinners and unbelievers, and if we are not Christians, he is our father. He is the father we should immediately divorce and walk away from as soon as we have the knowledge of God and his redeeming feature.

As long as a black father remains an unbeliever, he will never be in a position to be the father God has called him to be to his children, nor will he ever be able to please God. Until he accepts the redemption and love of Christ, he will remain as a blind man trying to lead the blind. Nothing is more rewarding than satisfying your father. However, as long as we live in the flesh, it will be impossible to please God.

Romans 8:8-17

So then, they that are in the flesh cannot please God. [9] But ye are not in the flesh, but in the Spirit, if so be that the Spirit of God dwell in you. Now if any man have not the Spirit of Christ, he is none of his. [10] And if Christ be in you, the body is dead because of sin; but the Spirit is life because of righteousness. [11] But if the Spirit of him that raised up Jesus from the dead dwell in you, he that raised up Christ from the dead shall also quicken your mortal bodies by his Spirit that dwelleth in you. [12]Therefore, brethren, we are debtors, not to the flesh, to live after the flesh.

[13] For if ye live after the flesh, ye shall die: but if ye through the Spirit do mortify the deeds of the body, ye shall live. [14] For as many as are led by the Spirit of God, they are the sons of God. [15] For ye have not received the spirit of bondage again to fear; but ye have received the Spirit of adoption, whereby we cry, Abba, Father. [16] The Spirit itself beareth witness with our spirit, that we are the children of God: [17] And if children, then heirs; heirs of God, and joint- heirs with Christ; if so be that we suffer with him, that we may be also glorified together.

When we set our eyes on the things of God, we can rejoice according to Luke 10:19-20, "Behold, I give unto you power to tread on serpents and scorpions, and over all the power of the enemy: and nothing shall by any means hurt you. [20] Notwithstanding in this rejoice not, that the spirits are subject unto you; but rather rejoice because your names are written in heaven." When we meditate on these scriptures, our desire for worldly possessions will begin to fade away.

The eighth chapter of the Gospel of John provides scriptures that can build a spiritual foundation for any father who desires a life built on truth. These scriptures reveal to us the real Father and the father of lies that dwells among us today.

John 8:36-46
If the Son, therefore, shall make you free, ye shall be free indeed. [37] I know that ye are Abraham's seed; but ye seek to kill me, because my word hath no place in you. [38] I speak that which I have seen with my Father: and ye do that which ye have seen with your father. [39] They answered and said unto him, Abraham is our father. Jesus saith unto them, If ye were Abraham's children, ye would do the works of Abraham. [40] But now ye seek to kill me, a man

39

that hath told you the truth, which I have heard of God: this did not Abraham. [41] Ye do the deeds of your father. Then said they to him, We be not born of fornication; we have one Father, even God. [42] Jesus said unto them, If God were your Father, ye would love me: for I proceeded forth and came from God; neither came I of myself, but he sent me. [43] Why do ye not understand my speech? even because ye cannot hear my word. [44] Ye are of your father the devil, and the lusts of your father ye will do. He was a murderer from the beginning, and abode not in the truth, because there is no truth in him. When he speaketh a lie, he speaketh of his own: for he is a liar, and the father of it. [45] And because I tell you the truth, ye believe me not. [46] Which of you convinceth me of sin? And if I say the truth, why do ye not believe me?

God's Word in 1 John 3 reveals to all of us who our father is and who it is that we serve, based on what we believe and how we live in this world. It is just as important for our African American children to know who their father is as it is for us as Christians to know God as our Father.

1 John 3:9-11
Whosoever is born of God doth not commit sin; for his seed remaineth in him: and he cannot sin, because he is born of God. [10] In this the children of God are manifest, and the children of the devil: whosoever doeth not righteousness is not of God, neither he that loveth not his brother. [11] For this is the message that ye heard from the beginning, that we should love one another.

As children of God, it is imperative for us to share our heritage in Christ with our families, so no matter what anyone in this world does or says, we know who we are according to Galatians 3.

Galatians 3:26-29
For ye are all the children of God by faith in Christ Jesus. [27] For as many of you as have been baptized into Christ have put on Christ. [28]There is neither Jew nor Greek, there is neither bond nor free, there is neither male nor female: for ye are all one in Christ Jesus. [29] And if ye be Christ's, then are ye Abraham's seed, and heirs according to the promise.

We can now find ourselves in a relationship with the Father that loves us so much that He gave His only son to die for us, so that we might live and have everlasting life. We now have a Father in our life that loves us unconditionally and will never leave nor forsake us. We now have a Father we can trust, a Father who will never lie, and the Father who will never break a promise. We have a Father who will provide for all of our needs and bless us with the desires of our hearts. Who would not want to have a Father like this?

Nevertheless, there are numerous households with absent fathers. The question is; what causes a father to be absent from the lives of his children? Everyone seems to have an opinion or some question as to why African-American fathers are absent from their children lives and household. Some of the most recent and popular ones are quoted from "The Absent Father Causes" Blog.[18]

I am not even going to try to sugarcoat this; I would like to understand why so many African-American fathers are totally absent? My ex-girlfriend just had a

[18] Guy Corneau, *Absent Fathers, Lost Sons.* The Search for Masculine Identity. (Boston, Massachusetts: Shambhala Publications, Inc; 1991), 38.

baby; she is five months now; I am not even the father of this child, but I love her child as if she was mine. I cannot think of something more unnatural and bizarre than not having any feelings towards something that is half yours, something you helped to create. I cannot even describe how much joy this baby has brought into her life. She lives three hours away and every time I drive up there, I am so looking forward to seeing this beautiful child. I think being attached to a child, is one of the most human or "humane" impulses, I cannot even understand rationally how some people can have no feelings towards or interest in their own children, absolutely bizarre![19]

An increasing number of quantitative and qualitative research find that of men who become fathers through non-marital births, black men are least likely (when compared to white and Hispanic fathers) to marry or cohabit with the mother (Mott 1994; Lerman and Sorensen 2000). But they were found to have the highest rates (estimates range from 20 percent to over 50 percent) of visitation or provision of some caretaking or in-kind support (more than formal child support). For instance, Carlson and McLanahan's (2002) figures indicated that only 37 percent of black non-marital fathers were cohabiting with the child (compared to 66 percent of white fathers and 59 percent of Hispanic), but of those who weren't cohabiting, 44 percent of unmarried black fathers were visiting the child, compared to only 17 percent of white and 26 percent of Hispanic fathers. These studies also suggested that black nonresident fathers tend to maintain their level of involvement over time longer than do white and Hispanic nonresident fathers (Danziger and Radin

---

[19] http://www.city-data.com/forum/politics-other-controversies/1593583-absent-black-father-causes.html

1990; Taylor et al. 1990; Seltzer 1991; Stier and Tienda 1993; Wattenberg 1993; Coley and Chase-Lansdale 1999).[20]

While it would be remiss to argue that there are not many absent black fathers, absence is only one slice of the fatherhood pie and a smaller slice than is normally thought. The problem with "absence," as is fairly well established now is that it is an ill-defined pejorative concept usually denoting non-residence with the child, and it is sometimes assumed in cases where there is no legal marriage to the mother. More importantly, absence connotes invisibility and noninvolvement, which further investigation has proven to be exaggerated. Furthermore, statistics on children's living arrangements also indicate that nearly 41 percent of black children live with their fathers, either in a married or cohabiting couple household or with a single dad.[21]

Many noteworthy causes and opinions of absent fathers are discussed and identified in Table 3 "Bloggers' Opinions and Quotes," as to what they believe are the causes of absent fathers.

---

[20] http://www.city-data.com/forum/politics-other-controversies/1593583-absent-black-father-causes.html

[21] Ibid.

TABLE 3 THE ABSENT FATHER OPINION AND QUOTES[22]

Blogger Number	Bloggers' Opinions and Quotes
1.	"Uncle Sam does a decent job of taking care of the kids even if the mother is poor and in debt by providing free day care (or very low cost) job assistance programs, and a host of other benefits."
2.	"Society, today, is very social, women are hunted like deer; a good looking woman is approached by several men a day, so she has options, plenty of options to find a man."
3.	"Money is primarily a replacement for love to a lot of women, women in general are more infatuated with a man's income than a man is into her income, lots of black men aren't trying to abandon the child but financially they can't help much. Salary wise, black men are about $10 behind on average compared to white men. One can blame the lack of efforts, but racism and stereotyping plays a big part of that, black men rarely look professional to many of white America."
4.	"Black culture, if you look closely has integrated itself into white culture, black women want to experience the "good life" like a lot of white women do, they want a man with a good job, stable, vacations and so forth. So many black men may have a child with a woman, but he is so poor that he is considered a bum, and she decides to leave him and just find a better man who can do a better job providing."

[22] Ibid.

Blogger Number	Bloggers' Opinions and Quotes
5.	"Money is everything in America and a relationship is primarily business, cold but true; black men are on the bottom. While looks and aggression can get a man into bed, it can't make the women love him for life and stick with him when he's down on his luck."
6.	"Most breakups are caused by women not men. Black women just are not happy and want to move on, it is hard to date with a child by another man, most men aren't mature enough to handle that, and society made it that way."

Statistics have shown that some fathers who have children under the age of five years old living apart from them are involved in their lives with some day-to-day activities that allow them to bond with them. Figure 6 shows the percentage of fathers that read, played with, bathed, dressed, diapered,

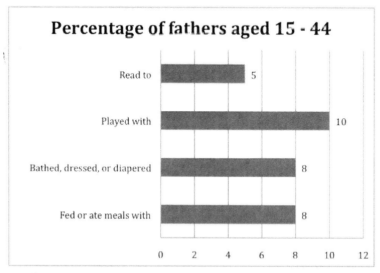

Figure 6. Children under age five years living apart from fathers.

and fed their children. These activities are meaningful to both mother and child. They are activities that can strengthen the relationship of a divided family.

Similarly, the statistics shown in Figure 7 show the importance of a father's involvement beyond age five (ages 5 to 18). The involvement of activities changes between the ages of 5 to 18 to helping with homework, talking about their day, taking them to activities, and having a meal with them. However, the key to an absent father being in a position to continue in the lives of his children is highly dependent upon the relationship he has with the mother and his documented legal rights. Without any legal documents in place, African-American mothers have been accused of being vindictive by keeping the father away from their children. Because they are unable to maintain a relationship with the father, they despise the idea of the father of their children being in a relation-ship with another female. However, once they can establish a promising relationship with another man, the door of avail-ability to see the children reopens to the father.

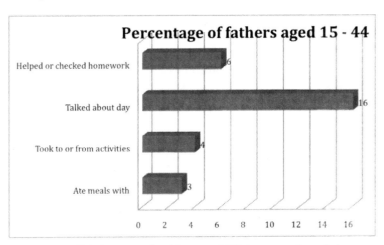

Figure 7. Children ages 5 – 18 years old living apart from fathers.

3. A FATHER'S PRESENCE

The presence of a father in the life of his children is priceless. There is no monetary value that one can place on the relationship of a father and his children. It is so critical to the life and development of a child. A child does not choose his father; it is a birth event that one has to live with for a lifetime. However, it should be noted that there are some children whose lives would be more productive and enjoyable if the father who is present "in the body only" would leave. If the father's presence is based on obligation only, and love and compassion for the child is absent in the relationship, there is a strong potential for abuse and abandonment issues to surface later in the child's life. Simply put, it would be better for the child and the father if the father would either step up to the plate or leave. I know that this statement sounds harsh, but being a father is not doing things out of obligation and responsibility; it is doing things out of love and commitment, because of a committed relationship to the family.

Personally, I know the importance of having a father present in the home. As a child growing up, I have no memories of any other man other than my father. As far back as I can remember, my dad was always present in my life until the day he died. He was the one I looked to for counseling and direction. He was my mentor, not some professional athlete or Hollywood actor. I am not saying that he was perfect; none of us are perfect. I am saying that when I needed something, my father was the one I turned to; he was the one I depended on to provide what I needed. It did not matter what I needed. It could have been food, clothing, advice, counseling, money, or parental support. He was the first and the last person I looked for to meet those needs. I had no other options; as a child he was my only dependable choice.

Therefore, when I look back on some of the things that my dad did for me, I find it hard to imagine what it is like for a child growing up in today's society without a father at home. I do know a child growing up in today's society without a father will not experience the kind of support and love from a father that I enjoyed and received. I can remember the excitement of seeing my dad returning home from work after a long, exhausting day. I waited to share with him what was going on in my little world, with the exception of those days that I knew I had been disobedient, and my mom had promised me that as soon as my dad returned home from work, she was going to tell him and let him discipline me. Trust me, on those occasions I was not happy to see my dad, knowing chastisement was coming. Even in correction and disciplining, I knew my dad loved me and that the pain he was about to inflict upon my posterior was for my good. Regardless of the positive effects of such discipline, I was never receptive to receiving it from him.

God's Word has instructed us in Proverbs 19:18 to "chasten thy son while there is hope, and let not thy soul spare for his crying." Believe me, there was plenty of crying. Crying that did not phase my father in any way or convince him to stop whipping me. All of the disciplining I received from my father occurred while I was young, before I became a teenager. By the time I was a teenager, I knew my father's expectations of me. I also knew the consequences if I failed to meet his expectations in behavior, education, honor, respect, or responsibilities.

The disciplinary actions given to children that were once the sole responsibility of a father has shifted to mothers and the legal system. There are now laws and government agencies that tell parents what they can and cannot do in disciplining their children. I understand that there are parents who abuse their children, but no one knows how to discipline their child better than a parent. I cannot help but believe that if the statistics of fathers being fathers in their children's lives had stood the course of time in ~~African American~~ families, none of these laws would be necessary. It is the active presence and participation of a father in a child's life that makes the difference, not laws.

Noted sociologist Dr. David Popenoe is one of the pioneers of the relatively young field of research into fathers and fatherhood. He stated, "Fathers are far more than just 'second adults' in the home…Involved fathers bring positive benefits to their children that no other person is as likely to bring." [23]

One of the most important influences a father can have on his child is indirect; fathers influence their children in large part through the quality of their relationship with the mother of their children. A father who has a good relationship with the mother of his children is more likely to be involved with, and to spend time with, their children. He will be more likely to have children who are psychologically and emotionally healthy. Similarly, a mother who feels affirmed by her children's father and who enjoys the benefits of a happy relationship is more likely to be a better mother. Indeed, the quality of the relationship affects the parenting behavior of both parents. They are more responsive, affectionate, and confident with their infants; more self-controlled in dealing with defiant

[23] Popenoe, D. (1996). Life without father: http://www.citizenlink.org/ FOSI/marriage/A000002226.cfm

toddlers; and better confidants for teenagers seeking advice and emotional support. [24]

One of the most important benefits of a positive relationship between mother and father, and a benefit directly related to the objectives of the Child Protective Services (CPS) caseworker, is the behavior it models for children. Fathers who treat the mothers of their children with respect and deal with conflict within the relationship in an adult and appropriate manner, are more likely to have boys who understand how they are to treat women and who are less likely to act in an aggressive fashion toward females. Girls with involved, respectful fathers see how they should expect men to treat them and are less likely to become involved in violent or unhealthy relationships. In contrast, research has shown that husbands who display anger, show contempt for, or who stonewall their wives (i.e., "the silent treatment") are more likely to have children who are anxious, withdrawn, or antisocial. [25]

A number of studies suggest that fathers who are involved, nurturing, and playful with their infants have children with higher IQs, as well as better linguistic and cognitive capacities.[26] Toddlers with involved fathers go on to start school with higher levels of academic readiness. They are more patient and can handle the stresses and frustrations associated with schooling more readily than children with less involved fathers.[27]

The influence of a father's involvement on academic performance extends into adolescence and young adulthood. Numerous studies find that an active and nurturing style of

[24] Lamb, M. E. (1997). The role of fathers in child development (3rd ed., pp. 49-65, 318-325). New York, NY: John Wiley & Sons; Lamb, M. E.

[25] http://www.cdc.gov/nchs/data/nhsr/nhsr064.pdf.

[26] Ibid

[27] Ibid

fathering is associated with better verbal skills, intellectual functioning, and academic achievement among adolescents.[28] For instance, a 2001 U.S. Department of Education study found that highly involved biological fathers had children who were 43 percent more likely than other children to earn mostly A's and 33 percent less likely than other children to repeat a grade.[29]
 Even from birth, children who have an involved father are more likely to be emotionally secure, be confident to explore their surroundings and, as they grow older, have better social connections with peers. These children are also less likely to get in trouble at home, school, or in the neighborhood.[30] Infants who receive high levels of affection from their fathers (e.g., babies whose fathers respond quickly to their cries and who play together) are more securely attached; that is, they can explore their environment comfortably when a parent is nearby and can readily accept comfort from their parent after a brief separation. A number of studies suggest they are also more sociable and popular with other children throughout early childhood. [31]

The way fathers play with their children also has an important impact on a child's emotional and social development. Fathers spend a much higher percentage of their one-on-one interaction with infants and preschoolers in stimulating, playful activity than do mothers. From these interactions, children learn how to regulate their feelings and behavior. Roughhousing with dad, for example, can teach children how to deal with aggressive impulses and physical contact without losing control of their emotions.[32] Fathers also tend to promote

[28] http://nces.ed.gov/pubsearch/pubsinfo.asp?pubid=2001032.

[29] http://www.cdc.gov/nchs/data/nhsr/nhsr064.pdf.

[30] Ibid

[31] Ibid

[32] Ibid

independence and an orientation to the outside world. Fathers often push achievement while mothers stress nurturing, both of which are important to healthy development. As a result, children who grow up with involved fathers are more comfortable exploring the world around them and more likely to exhibit self-control and pro-social behavior. [33]

One study of school-aged children found that children with good relationships with their fathers were less likely to experience depression, to exhibit disruptive behavior, or to lie and were more likely to exhibit pro-social behavior.[34] This same study found that boys with involved fathers had fewer school behavior problems and that girls had stronger self-esteem.[35] In addition, many studies have found that children who live with their fathers are more likely to have good physical and emotional health, to achieve academically, and to avoid drugs, violence, and delinquent behavior. [36]

In short, fathers have a powerful and positive impact upon the development and health of their children. A caseworker who understands the important contributions fathers make to their children's development and how to effectively involve fathers in the case planning process will find additional and valuable allies in the mission to create a permanent and safe environment for children.[37]

The goal of these statistics in the following figures and tables are to document the extent of father involvement in their

---

[33] http://www.cdc.gov/nchs/data/nhsr/nhsr064.pdf

[34] Mosley, J., & Thompson, E. (1995). Fathering behavior and child outcomes: (pp. 148-165). Thousand Oaks, CA: Sage.

[35] Ibid

[36] Horn, W., & Sylvester, T. (2002); U. S. Department of Health and Human Services, Substance Abuse and Mental Health Services Administration (SAMHSA). (1996).

[37] http://www.cdc.gov/nchs/data/nhsr/nhsr064.pdf

children's lives using the sample of 3,928 fathers aged 15–44 in the 2006–2010 National Survey of Family Growth. While other surveys have collected data on father involvement in recent decades, the National Survey of Family Growth sample is large, recent, and nationally representative. It also has various indicators of father involvement for both fathers who live with their children and fathers who live apart from their children.[38]

The statistical data is limited to four measures of father involvement for children under age five years and to four measures of involvement for children aged 5–18 years. Identical measures were compared for fathers aged 15–44 who lived with and who lived apart from their children. Parental involvement is complex and multidimensional. The measures selected for the study and examined here were chosen because previous research has found them to be related to positive outcomes for children. Multiple indicators are shown because no one indicator is the key father-involvement activity that benefits all children more than others.[39]

Some of the findings shown here are worth reiterating, as there was variation in father involvement by activity. For example, for children under age five, the study found that 96% of resident fathers ate meals with their children every day or several times a week; 98% played with their children often; 90% bathed, diapered, or dressed their children every day or several times a week, and 60% read to their children that often. For the fathers who did not live with their children, 30% ate meals with them every day or several times a week; 39% played with their children several times a week or more; 31% bathed, diapered, or dressed their children several times a week or more, and 23% read to their children several times a week or more.[40]

---

[38] http://www.cdc.gov/nchs/data/nhsr/nhsr064.pdf

[39] Ibid

[40] Ibid

Variation in the frequency of activities was also evident among fathers with school-aged children (aged 5–18). For fathers who lived with these children, 93% ate meals with their children, and 92.5% talked with these children about things that happened during their day several times a week or every day. This compares with 63% of fathers who helped with or checked homework and 55% of fathers who took these children to or from activities.[41]

The 2006–2010 National Survey of Family Growth data has several limitations in examining father involvement. First, only men aged 15–44 were included in the study, limiting what can be said about involvement with their children by fathers aged 45 and over. Involvement may differ among these fathers compared with fathers aged 15–44, but these statistics found very few differences by age in the level of involvement in activities. The differences by age that were found suggest that older fathers may be less involved than fathers aged 15–44 in their children's lives, especially fathers with non co-residential children aged 0–4.[42]

A second limitation is that the father involvement questions were not asked for a particular, focal child if fathers had more than one co-residential or non co-residential child in the age range. It is not clear, then, how these fathers responded if they had different levels of involvement with the different children. For example, if a man lived with a 6-month-old baby and a 3-yearold child, and he spent more time with the child than with the baby, it is not possible to know whether he "averaged" the time he spent with each child or answered questions in regard to just one.[43]

---

[41] http://www.cdc.gov/nchs/data/nhsr/nhsr064.pdf

[42] Ibid

[43] http://www.cdc.gov/nchs/data/nhsr/nhsr064.pdf

Another limitation of the 2006–2010 National Survey of Family Growth was the relatively small number of measures across dimensions of father involvement. In response to these limitations National Survey of Family Growth, which began interviewing in September 2011, was redesigned to include multiple measures of more dimensions of father involvement and to ask these questions about a specific, focal child within each residence category. In this redesigned study, the youngest co-residential and the youngest non co-residential children are selected as the focal children when fathers are asked how often they engage in the father-involvement activities. The redesign and the addition of many questions will allow researchers to examine father involvement in more depth than was possible here.[44]

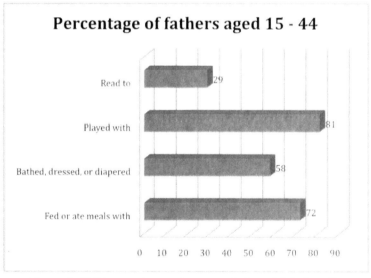

Figure 8. Children under age five years living with fathers.[45]

---

[44] Ibid

[45] http://www.cdc.gov/nchs/data/nhsr/nhsr064.pdf

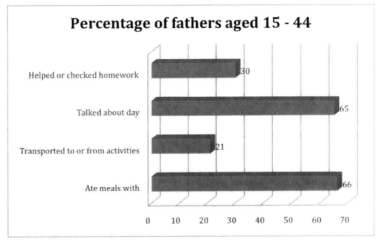

Figure 9. Children ages 5 – 18 years old living with fathers.[46]

When the fathers of African-American children begin to seek the face of God and His divine direction on how to raise their children with Christian principles, they will soon come to the realization that God expects men to be fathers in a family environment and structure, as defined by His Word. It does not matter what the world says or does. It is all about what the Word of God says and what He expects from His people. What a difference it will make in the homes of our African-American families when this kind of commitment becomes a daily lifestyle. It should ignite the African-American family to serve and trust God with a sincere heart. In addition, it will ignite fathers to become the role models their children are looking for in a lost and confused world.

---

[46] http://www.cdc.gov/nchs/data/nhsr/nhsr064.pdf

4. TODAY'S AFRICAN-AMERICAN FAMILY STRUCTURE

African-American families today have taken a step backward in their spiritual beliefs and Christian commitments to the Lord. As African-Americans ᴬˢ ᴴᵁᴹᴬᴺˢ, we find ourselves in a position where we are laboring in vain, because the houses we have built do not include the Lord and we are not building to His blueprints: the Word of God, Psalms 127.

> Psalms 127:1-5
> Except the LORD build the house, they labour in vain that build it: except the LORD keep the city, the watchman waketh but in vain.[2] It is vain for you to rise up early, to sit up late, to eat the bread of sorrows: for so he giveth his beloved sleep. [3] Lo, children are an heritage of the LORD: and the fruit of the womb is his reward. [4] As arrows are in the hand of a mighty man; so are children of the youth. [5] Happy is the man that hath his quiver full of them: they shall not be ashamed, but they shall speak with the enemies in the gate.

Satan knows that if he is going to disrupt our ability to manage our households well, he has to disrupt the order and cause confusion and dissension around us. Satan knows that whatever he can divide, he can dominate. The reason he disrupts us is because he knows that God operates in the context of unity. Satan seeks to remove God from the equation by dividing those under His rule. One of the major ways that Satan seeks to do this is through a woman's life by destroying the alignment that God has established.

When God created man and woman, He established an alignment between Himself and them, as well as between genders. Eve was created as a counterpart or helper to Adam, with Adam in a position of ultimate responsibility. Many women today are living under the strain of chaos because they are not positioned in their prescribed lanes to enjoy all that God has intended for them. Not only does this affect them, but it affects those around them as well.[47]

We have conformed to the ways of the world and failed to do what the Word of God directs us to do. Therefore, we find ourselves today living in houses with no godly presence, reverence, love, or fear of God. We live in cities not kept by the Lord, but by the enemy of this world. We are more concerned today with what the majority of the people want, instead of what the Word of God says. The problem with this is the majority does not care what the Word of God has to say about sin.

Our children are a blessing from God, and they deserve more than what we are offering and giving. They deserve the right to know the truth, so that they may be free. They can be free from the stronghold of sin, death, and a broken family structure where fathers are absent and uncaring.

As Christian parents, it is a major battle to establish and maintain a godly household. If anyone has told you that it is easy being a Christian parent, he did not tell you the truth.

---

[47] Tony Evans and Chrystal Evans Hurst. *Kingdom Woman.* (Carol Stream, Illinois: Tyndale House Publishers, Inc.; 2013), 155.

Remind them that our dedication and obedience to our flesh had a huge start on our new spirit man. Our flesh is always in a continuous fight with our spirit, and if our spirit is weak, our flesh will win the battles.

God is not asking us to do what is easy or quick. I know that is our mindset; that if something is easy or quick, we are quick to do it. That is not what God is asking us to do. What God is asking us to do is neither quick nor easy, but it is what He wants. Obedience to God is rewarding, profitable and what He expects.

It was not easy for the rich man to give up his riches to follow Jesus. When we hold on to things in this world, it is not easy for us to walk away from them and follow Jesus. Yes, we are following Jesus, but not a hundred percent. In fact, what have we left behind to follow Him, so that we can be the parents God has called us to be to our children?

Mark 10:25-31
It is easier for a camel to go through the eye of a needle, than for a rich man to enter into the kingdom of God. [26] And they were astonished out of measure, saying among themselves, Who then can be saved? [27] And Jesus looking upon them saith, With men it is impossible, but not with God: for with God all things are possible. [28] Then Peter began to say unto him, Lo, we have left all, and have followed thee. [29] And Jesus answered and said, Verily I say unto you, There is no man that hath left house, or brethren, or sisters, or father, or mother, or wife, or children, or lands, for my sake, and the gospel's, [30] But he shall receive an hundredfold now in this time, houses, and brethren, and sisters, and mothers, and children, and lands, with persecutions; and in the world to come eternal life. [31] But many that are first shall be last; and the last first.

Things that are easy to acquire are usually meaningless, insignificant, and shortly lived. Philippians 4:13, "I can do all things through Christ, which strengthened me."

Yes, we can do all things through Christ, which strengthened us, but we have to remember that it is through Christ. He has to strengthen us, because we are too weak and powerless to do things on our own. Jesus never intended for us to do it on our own, anyway.

Let us be honest. It is not easy to walk in obedience when the other option is easy and has the appearance of being more satisfying. More often than not, we choose to take the path of the easy alternative that is staring us in the face, because what we see requires no faith. It is easy to love those that love us. It is easy to forgive those that forgive us. It is easy to give to those who give back to us. It is easy to communicate with those who look and act like us. It is easy to get our shout and praise on when everything is going right in our families, and we have no trials and tribulations in our homes. Easy or not, God's expectations for African-Americans are no different from His expectations for any other human beings. He expects all humans to love, to forgive, to trust Him, and to walk in obedience.

However, what happens in our African-American families when there is adversity? What happens when something goes wrong? What happens when we find out that we are not in control? What happens when there is nothing we can do to change the situation? It all depends on the foundation you are standing on at the time of your adversity.

As an African-American, I do not know the weight of other families' crosses. I do not know how much other families are carrying and how much they are bearing. I do not understand how much a family is going through from day to day and how they have to stand on the Word of God and trust Him and His promises. Until I carry their cross or walk in their shoes, I will never understand.

However, what I do understand is that as African-Americans, we have to go back to the basics; the basic things that kept the family strong and moving in the right direction. We had a foundation where it was normal to bear one another's burdens and follow Galatians 6:2, "Bear ye one another's burdens, and so fulfil the law of Christ." There was a Christian foundation built in accordance with Romans 12.

Romans 12:14-18
Bless them which persecute you: bless, and curse not. |15| Rejoice with them that do rejoice, and weep with them that weep. |16| Be of the same mind one toward another. Mind not high things, but condescend to men of low estate. Be not wise in your own conceits. |17| Recompense to no man evil for evil. Provide things honest in the sight of all men. |18| If it be possible, as much as be in you, live peaceably with all men.

A majority of African-American children are born into single-parent homes. Compared to white women, black women are more likely to become teenage mothers, stay single and have marital instability, and are thus much more likely to live in female-headed, single-parent homes. This pattern has been coined as black matriarchy because of the observance of many households headed by women. The issue was first brought to national attention in 1965 by sociologist and later Democrat Senator Daniel Patrick Moynihan, in the groundbreaking Moynihan Report (also known as "The Negro Family: The Case for National Action"). Moynihan's report made the argument that the relative absence of nuclear families (those having both a father and mother present) in black America would greatly hinder further black socioeconomic progress.[48]

---

[48] http://en.m.wikipedia.org/wiki/African-American_family_structure

61

The current most widespread African-American family structure consisting of single parents has historical roots, dating back to 1880. Data from U.S. Census reports reveals that between 1880 and 1960, married households consisting of two-parent homes were the most widespread form of African-American family structures. Although the most popular, married households decreased over this time-period. Single-parent homes, on the other hand, remained relatively stable until 1960, when they rose dramatically. A study of 1880 family structures in Philadelphia showed that three-fourths of black families were nuclear families, composed of two parents and children.[49]

In New York City in 1925, 85% of kin-related black households had two parents. When Moynihan warned in his 1965 report of the coming destruction of the black family, however, the out-of-wedlock birthrate had increased to 25% among blacks. This figure continued to rise over time and in 1991, 68% of black children were born outside of marriage. U.S. Census data from 2010 reveals that more African-American families consisted of single-parent mothers than married homes with both parents. Most recently, in 2011, it was reported that 72% of black babies were born to unwed mothers.[50]

It is not easy, seeing how far we as African-Americans have fallen spiritually. It will be hard getting back to a solid foundation, but it is possible. We have to be prepared to fight to keep the faith. 1 Timothy 6:12 says, "Fight the good fight of faith, lay hold on eternal life, whereunto thou art also called, and hast professed a good profession before many witnesses." We need to be ready, as Timothy was instructed.

---

[49] Ibid

[50] http://en.m.wikipedia.org/wiki/African-American_family_structure

2 Timothy 4:6-8
For I am now ready to be offered, and the time of my departure is at hand. [7] I have fought a good fight, I have finished my course, I have kept the faith: [8] Henceforth there is laid up for me a crown of righteousness, which the Lord, the righteous judge, shall give me at that day: and not to me only, but unto all them also that love his appearing.

I believe God's Word in 2 Chronicles 7:14, "If My people who are called by My name will humble themselves, and pray and seek My face, and turn from their wicked ways, then I will hear from heaven, and will forgive their sin and heal their land." It is time for us to be humble and realize there is nothing we can do without Christ. We need to confess our sins and begin to build on the family foundation that was established hundreds of years ago. We are not as wise as we think we are and now find ourselves in a position where we believe the lies of this world instead of the truth of God's Word.

Romans 1:22 –25
Professing to be wise, they became fools, [23] and changed the glory of the incorruptible God into an image made like corruptible man—and birds and four-footed animals and creeping things. [24] Therefore God also gave them up to uncleanness, in the lusts of their hearts, to dishonor their bodies among themselves, [25] who exchanged the truth of God for the lie, and worshiped and served the creature rather than the Creator, who is blessed forever. Amen.

The rate of the African-American marriage is not only consistently lower than white Americans, but is also declining. These trends are so pervasive that families who are married are considered a minority family structure for blacks. In 1970, 64% of adult African-Americans were married. This rate was cut in half by 2004, when 32% of adult African-Americans were married. Conversely, in 2004, 45% of African-Americans had never been married, compared to only 25% of white Americans.[51]

While research has shown that marriage rates have dropped for African-Americans, the birth rate has not. Thus, the number of single-parent homes has risen dramatically for black women. One reason for the low rate of African-American marriages is the high marriage age of first-time marriages for many African-Americans. For African-American women, the marriage rate increases with age compared to white Americans who follow the same trends but marry at younger ages than African-Americans.[52]

One study found that the average age of marriage for black women with a high school degree was 21.8 years compared to 20.8 years for white women. Fewer labor force opportunities and a decline in real earnings for black males since 1960 are also named as a source of increasing marital instability. As some researchers argue, these two trends have led to a pool of fewer desirable male partners and thus resulted in more divorces.[53]

One type of marriage that has declined is the shotgun marriage. Shotgun marriages were performed on demand in the black community when a young man impregnated the daughter of another man. This drop in rate is documented by the amount of out-of-wedlock births that now commonly occur. Between 1965 and 1989, three-fourths of white out-of-wedlock births and three-fifths of black out-of-wedlock births

[51] http://en.m.wikipedia.org/wiki/African-American_family_structure

[52] Ibid

[53] http://en.m.wikipedia.org/wiki/African-American_family_structure

could be explained by situations where the parents would have married in the past. Prior to the 1970s the norm was, should a couple have a pregnancy out of wedlock, marriage was inevitable. Cultural norms have since changed, giving women and men more agencies to decide whether or when they should get married.[54]

African-Americans have always preached and taught on the importance of marriage and strong families. At one point in our culture, having babies before marriage and not considering marriage was a disgrace. Those teachings were so deeply rooted in me that I felt like a complete failure and embarrassment to my family after the failure of my first marriage.

For African-Americans who do marry, the rate of divorce is higher than white Americans. While the trend is the same for both African-Americans and white Americans, with at least half of marriages for the two groups ending in divorce, the rate of divorce tends to be consistently higher for African-Americans. African-Americans also tend to spend less time married than white Americans. Overall, African-Americans are married at a later age, spend less time married, and are more likely to be divorced than white Americans.[55]

The decline and low success rate of black marriages is crucial for study because many African-Americans achieve a middle-class status through marriage and the likelihood for children to grow up in poverty triples for those in single parent rather than two-parent homes. Some researchers suggest that the reason for the rise in divorce rates is the increasing acceptability of divorces. The decline in social stigma of divorce has led to a decrease in the number of legal barriers of getting a divorce, thus making it easier for couples

---

[54] Ibid

[55] http://en.m.wikipedia.org/wiki/African-American_family_structure

to divorce.[56] The words "separation" and "divorce" should never be invited into a home.

I have been married twice; the first time I was not a born again Christian and neither was my wife. We had a marriage that was very absent and void of godly principles, with no Christian relatives to lead the way or set an example. Her parents were divorced, and my father was "old school." Old school means that he believed that as long as he provided a home, food, clothing, and money, his marriage was a success, and he answered to no one. So as you can see, neither my wife nor I had a good example to follow.

As a result, I begin my first marriage as a selfish, inconsiderate, critical, judgmental, non-supportive, and verbally abusive husband to my wife with no regrets or remorse for my behavior. I only cared about what made me happy in marriage. I thought I could change my wife to be what I wanted and expected from a wife. I never considered what she wanted. This led to a divorce after three tough and stressful years of marriage. One may have thought that it was my wife who gave up on our marriage and filed for a divorce. However, it was not my wife, it was I. I initiated the divorce. I filed the divorce papers, and I rejected counseling. I had no interest in working things out. I just wanted out, so I got out. I learned that "I" is a selfish and destructive word when used frequently in marriage.

You may be wondering why I am discussing my first marriage and my ex-wife in a book that should be on the wife that I have now. The explanation is in my testimony. My ex-wife, my first wife for three years, is also my current wife of almost 24 years. This one thing I know: only God has the power to take something that was broken and destroyed for eight years and restore it to something that is better, stronger, more exciting, and more solid than the original.

---

[56] Ibid

Eight years is a long time to be divorced and more than enough time to find another spouse and start a new family. Why would I consider returning to a relationship and marriage that was broken? Because God instructed me to do so and it was confirmed through a Word of prophecy from a woman of God. I wanted to reconcile with my wife during the first two years of our divorce, but after that my heart hardened and I wanted nothing to do with her (in fact, my heart was so hard that I no longer liked her). Therefore, for the next five years, I found myself in and out of relationships, beds, hotels, cruise ships, vacations, and business trips with numerous women. I had abandoned marriage and family to become a traveling whore, looking for love in all the wrong places.

During my eight years of divorce from my wife, I lived a wild life in and out of relationships and beds with many women, many in the same day. These were women who were looking for love and a husband. However, all I wanted was pleasure and freedom from any resemblance of a committed relationship. It was only because of God's grace and mercy that no woman killed me for using her. It is a miracle that I did not contract AIDS or any STD or have illegitimate chil dren. I know someone was praying for me. Prayers that I was not aware of at the time got me through some tough times in my life.

Meanwhile, four years into our divorce I moved to Fort Lauderdale, Florida to accept a management position with a power supply company. During the first year in south Florida, I continued my sinful habits. However, something happened in the second year; I begin to feel empty after five years of trying to satisfy this fleshly body.

Not long after I moved to Ft. Lauderdale, one of my employees who was an evangelist and the wife of an assistant pastor invited me to a Friday night church service. I accepted the invitation. I enjoyed it so much that I returned on Sunday. On that Sunday after the pastor preached the Word of God, he extended an invitation to sinners to accept Christ and I heard within my spirit the Lord calling me to repentance. Minutes later the pastor said, "The Lord is calling someone Now. Do not resist the Lord's calling, and come now." Nevertheless, I could not move from my pew; it was as if something stronger than me was holding me in the pew. A few minutes later, another man went forth, and I was left in awe, thinking that I had heard the Lord calling this man in my spirit to repentance.

When I returned the next Sunday, I heard the same calling. This time there was no man going forth; and I was able to leave my pew after fighting with my flesh. I will never forget that day. The pastor had me pray a prayer of repentance and confess Jesus Christ as Lord of my life. As I prayed, the Lord showed me who I was, a sinner. I cried uncontrollably and wondered who could ever love a sinner like me. I could hear in my spirit the Lord saying to me, "I forgive you and I love you, my son." I accepted Jesus that day and I have never looked back.

Consequently, I ended my whorish ways after that day and became a Christian and a faithful member of the ministry. I later shared my testimony with my ex-wife, but she did not believe me. I thought she would see me differently. She did not believe a word of it. She said I was still a whore and a cheater. I told her that I was in a relationship with Jesus and that I could not cheat on Him, because He sees everything I do and knows my every thought. I told my ex-wife that I did not care if she ever believed me, because I was going to serve the Lord.

Meanwhile, when friends and family got word of my new changed life, they believed that my ex-wife and I would reconcile. Nevertheless, I wanted to marry someone else that I had dated for nearly five years. However, God would not release me to marry her. Whenever I prayed about marrying her, God would always place my ex-wife in my spirit. By then, I had lost interest in remarrying her. I wanted nothing else to do with her. In my mind, she was just the mother of my baby girl.

Admittedly, what comes to mind is the day that my former girlfriend and I discussed marriage. After we had gone away and prayed about it, both of us were shocked by the words we heard from God. She told me that God told her no, and that He was going to reconcile my ex-wife and me. I heard the same exact words from the Lord. We stopped dating after this and I decided not to date anyone. In fact, it was three years before my ex-wife believed that my life had changed and that I was a Christian.

Nevertheless, God spoke to my ex-wife and told her the same message He had told my ex-girlfriend and me. My ex-wife called me and told me what the Lord had told her. I am sure, even to this day, that it was the most difficult call she ever had to make. She asked me if I still wanted to remarry her. She told me that she was not in love with me and that she was being obedient to what the Lord had asked her to do. I replied by telling her that I was not in love with her either, but I was willing to remarry her and reconcile my family. At the time, my son was living with me and my daughter was living with her.

During those three years of waiting and praying for a wife, I knew that I had family and friends praying for my family and me. During Christmas of that year, I presented my ex-wife with an engagement ring. She placed it on hand with a big smile and we remarried in March 1991. We have now been happily married for 23 years and counting. The words "separation" and "divorce" are not a part of our vocabulary; with the two of us it is "until death do us part."

Why is this testimony important? Because it personally shows a broken foundation, lies, sins, pride, reconciliation, healing, re-birth, forgiveness, love, trust, and Jesus. In other words, this testimony consists of everything that can destroy a family structure from a marriage viewpoint and everything that is required for a strong family to succeed.

God desires to build a testimony in each of us. Each of us is one of God's chosen vessels to reflect His power in and through us. When others read, hear, or see this power reflected, they are impacted because they cannot explain that power. I cannot explain a divorce that spanned over eight years and ended in reconciliation. It was a second chance at marriage with the same wife that has now lasted over 23 years. All I know is that God desires to frame our lives with experiences designed to reflect the character and nature of Christ. Sometimes these events can be very devastating, but they are designed to reveal His power in and through us when we trust Him.

Life is living with the choices we make. We can point our fingers at our parents, our culture, our loved ones, or the one we love, but the bottom line is that we are accountable for our decisions and our sins. We need to own our decisions, as well as own and confess our sins, if we want to see reconciliation and restoration. As men and leaders, it is time out for blaming Satan and women for our sinful decisions. By now, we should have learned something from Genesis 3.

Genesis 3:1-13
Now the serpent was more subtil than any beast of the field which the Lord God had made. And he said unto the woman, Yea, hath God said, Ye shall not eat of every tree of the garden? [2] And the woman said unto the serpent, We may eat of the fruit of the trees of the garden: [3] But of the fruit of the tree which is in the midst of the garden, God hath said, Ye shall not eat of it, neither shall ye touch it, lest ye die.[4] And the serpent said unto the woman, Ye shall not surely die: [5] For God doth know that in the day ye eat thereof, then your eyes shall be opened, and ye shall

be as gods, knowing good and evil. [6] And when the woman saw that the tree was good for food, and that it was pleasant to the eyes, and a tree to be desired to make one wise, she took of the fruit thereof, and did eat, and gave also unto her husband with her; and he did eat. [7] And the eyes of them both were opened, and they knew that they were naked; and they sewed fig leaves together, and made themselves aprons. [8] And they heard the voice of the Lord God walking in the garden in the cool of the day: and Adam and his wife hid themselves from the presence of the Lord God amongst the trees of the garden. [9] And the Lord God called unto Adam, and said unto him, Where art thou? [10] And he said, I heard thy voice in the garden, and I was afraid, because I was naked; and I hid myself. [11] And he said, Who told thee that thou wast naked? Hast thou eaten of the tree, whereof I commanded thee that thou shouldest not eat? [12] And the man said, The woman whom thou gavest to be with me, she gave me of the tree, and I did eat. [13] And the Lord God said unto the woman, What is this that thou hast done? And the woman said, The serpent beguiled me, and I did eat.

When we look throughout the scriptures, we find that God is constantly teaching us lessons on obedience, trust, and faith. Therefore, we do not have to be the Moses of today, frustrated, agitated, and angry at the sins and downfall of the African-American families. We need to listen to the voice of God and walk in obedience with the determination to make a difference, one family at a time.

Numbers 20:7-12
And the Lord spake unto Moses, saying, [8] Take the rod, and gather thou the assembly together, thou, and

Aaron thy brother, and speak ye unto the rock before their eyes; and it shall give forth his water, and thou shalt bring forth to them water out of the rock: so thou shalt give the congregation and their beasts drink. [9] And Moses took the rod from before the Lord, as he commanded him. [10] And Moses and Aaron gathered the congregation together before the rock, and he said unto them, Hear now, ye rebels; must we fetch you water out of this rock? [11] And Moses lifted up his hand, and with his rod he smote the rock twice: and the water came out abundantly, and the congregation drank, and their beasts also. [12] And the Lord spake unto Moses and Aaron, Because ye believed me not, to sanctify me in the eyes of the children of Israel, therefore ye shall not bring this congregation into the land which I have given them.

There is a parental responsibility for black fathers to strengthen and celebrate the link between themselves, their children, and God. Purposefully placing our children in His direct, divine path is a responsibility second to none. Fathers hold a unique responsibility. Not sole responsibility, mind you (because the mother quite often assumes the role of religious anchor in the black unit) but a unique responsibility. It is the role a father should cherish and one, unfortunately, that is often overlooked or unrecognized in the rush of today's hectic world. Nevertheless, it will save and redirect our children's lives and strengthen the fabric of the black unit. The adage that "the family that prays together, stays together" is not merely a catchy jingle; it is miraculous in its intensity and accuracy.[57]

---

[57] Kristin Clark Taylor. Black Fathers A Call For Healing. (New York, New York: Doubleday; 2003), 36.

Our developing African-American communities will
be what shape the direction of our families and, indeed, our
futures. Ironically, integration and the civil rights struggle
of the sixties, as useful as they were at the time, simultaneously struck a harmful blow to the solidity and structural
integrity of the black family. Highways cut through communities. Busing brought along with it anxiety and separation.
Moving out to the suburbs; getting away from our people to
live "in comfort" with white people was how we began to
measure our success. Family dynamics began to change, and
with it divorce rates rose. Single-parent households became
more the norm than the exception. We were now more isolated from each other; our collective, communal values were
dangerously diminished. The only thing that kept us going,
unfortunately, that kept us moving and motivated, was trying
to get a bigger piece of the pie, even if it meant destroying
ourselves in the process.[58]

Ask any architect or design engineer: rebuilding a structure — whether it is a house, a skyscraper, or a community — is
infinitely easier if a strong, solid foundation has already been
laid; if we are already familiar with its dimensions, its depth,
its ability to stand, unyielding against the strongest winds of
adversity and change. As a race of people, we once had that
strong foundation. The question then becomes: Do we have
the tools, the driving desire, a vision, and the resources to
rebuild that foundation?[59]

Our decision to rebuild or not rebuild is not optional; it
is mandatory. Our survival depends on it. We alone are the
only ones who can manage the task. We alone have the shared
collective memories, the energy, the capital, and the vision
for a new and brighter day. There are already generations

---

[58] Kristin Clark Taylor. Black Fathers A Call For Healing. (New York,
New York: Doubleday; 2003), 108.

[59] Ibid. 112.

today who have no earthly idea of what a shared community is. However, we cannot blame them for their ignorance. We can only blame ourselves for not passing along to them the moral absolutes which we once abided by, and for allowing successive generations to be brought into this world with no sense of moral clarity.

Our families and communities are dwindling away at an alarming rate, almost into extinction. To survive, we must revive the notion of shared community and common concern; when one hurts, we all hurt. When one is in need, we all are in need.[60] When a young person is murdered unjustly by an opposite race, the entire community grieves and comes together. The problem with this is that there are more young people murdered through black on black crimes without an outcry from the black community. Crime is crime, and murder is murder, regardless of who commits it. It is a sin and should always be a grievous situation in all of our lives, regardless of race or color.

As African-Americans, blacks must learn to not only do what is right, but also do what is required, even if it means sacrificing for the common good of the community. We must be truly committed to the concept of reweaving the beautiful fabric of the black community; the communities we used to cherish. To do so, we must first acknowledge that this task cannot be performed alone or even in isolated pockets. Reliving warm memories costs us nothing. Re-creating some of the shared values and collective wisdom associated with those warm memories and redesigning our communities so that they are again cohesive safety nets will be staggeringly expensive, but it can be done.[61]

---

[60] Kristin Clark Taylor. Black Fathers A Call For Healing. (New York, New York: Doubleday; 2003), 112.

[61] Ibid. 125.

Furthermore, not only can this be done, it must be done. It does not matter where we live. We have the transportation to return and invest in our once thriving black communities. I do not mean to look to the city or government. I mean that, as blacks, we need to invest time and energy into our black communities. We are not that far removed that we cannot remember how African-American neighbors used to look out for one another. Now we live in our beautiful homes among neighbors who distance themselves from us and only speak to be polite.

5. STRUGGLES OF A SINGLE PARENT

Raising children as a single parent can be ultra-stressful, exhausting and a non-stop juggling act. Those navigating the parenting road without a partner can take some small comfort in knowing they are far from alone. Single moms and dads headed up nearly 12.3 million households in 2012, according to the U.S. Census Bureau, with single moms taking on the vast majority of the burden, caring for more than 10.3 million kids.[62]

The division of children between one and two-parent households appears to vary widely based on ethnicity. The Population Reference Bureau (PRB) report indicates about 16 percent of white children live with single moms, compared to 27 percent of Latino children and 52 percent of African-American children.[63]

Among the many challenges facing the millions of single parents are poverty, limited access to health insurance, difficulty securing affordable childcare, and lack of financial support from the absent parent. Despite the fact that 75 percent of single mothers are employed, the PRB reports 70 percent of children living with single moms are considered poor or

---

[62] http://everydaylife.globalpost.com/single-parents-4202.html

[63] Ibid

low-income. The parent's age, education level, and ability to secure a higher-paying job all influence the bottom line. In the U.S., more than half of low-income mothers are under age 34 and 61 percent lack a college education.[64]

The rising number of single father households from 1960 to 2011 is reflected in Figure 10. The numbers are based on household heads ages 15 and older who have children younger than 18 in the household. Fathers who are married but their spouse is absent, and those who are cohabiting with a non-marital partner are classified as single fathers. The trends show significant increases every ten years, which means each year the number of single-father households is increasing and not decreasing, climbing to heights never imagined.[65]

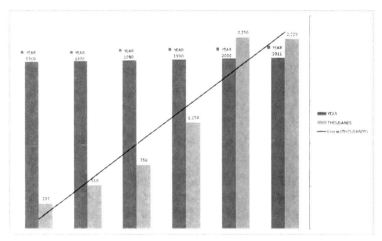

Figure 10. Rising number of single father households, 1960–2011.

The statistics are shocking; a single father heads a record 8% of households with minor children in the United States, up from just over 1% in 1960, according to a Pew Research Center analysis of Decennial Census and American

[64] Ibid

[65] http://www.pewsocialtrends.org/2013/07/02/the-rise-of-single-fathers/

Community Survey data. The number of single father households has increased about nine-fold since 1960, from less than 300,000 to more than 2.6 million in 2011. In comparison, the number of single mother households increased more than fourfold during that time, up to 8.6 million in 2011, from 1.9 million in 1960. As a result, men make up a growing share of single parent householders. In 1960, about 14% of single-parent households were headed by fathers; today almost one-quarter (24%) are headed by single fathers. [66]

There are some notable differences between single mothers and single fathers. Single fathers are more likely than single mothers to be living with a cohabiting partner (41% versus 16%). Single fathers, on average, have higher incomes than single mothers and are far less likely to be living at or below the poverty line (24% versus 43%). Single fathers are also somewhat less educated than single mothers, older and more likely to be white. Compared with fathers heading households with two married parents, single dads are younger, less educated, less financially well off and less likely to be white.[67]

Black fathers are the most likely to be heads of single father households; 29% are now in that position. This share drops to 20% among Hispanic fathers and just 14% among white fathers. The prevalence of single fatherhood is closely linked to educational level; the more education a father has, the less likely he is to head a single father household. While about one-fourth (26%) of fathers lacking a high school diploma are single fathers, the share drops to 22% for fathers with a high school degree. Among dads with some college, 17% are single fathers, and just 7% of fathers with a bachelor's degree fall into this category.[68]

---

[66] http://www.pewsocialtrends.org/2013/07/02/the-rise-of-single-fathers/

[67] Ibid

[68] Ibid

Some 27% of fathers under the age of 30 are single fathers, and most of these are cohabiting. The share of fathers that are single fathers declines markedly at older ages — 16% of those ages 30-39 are single fathers, and 13% of those ages 40 or older are single fathers. While the bulk of single fathers among younger men are cohabiting, the reverse is true for fathers ages 40 and older; most of these single fathers have no spouse or partner in their household. Poverty is also linked with single fatherhood; more than one-third (36%) of fathers who are living at or below the poverty line are single parents. This share drops to 13% for those living above the poverty line.[69]

One ethnographic researcher talked to single black fathers about their reasons for deciding to raise their children alone. They told the researcher that "they felt a sense of duty for their children that they wanted to avoid their own childhood experience of having a father absent, that they wanted to be a role model and that they felt a strong bond with their kids." These fathers had high expectations for their kids and got most of their parenting advice from their mothers. Most of the fathers reported that single parenting had a positive impact on their lives, and they felt the relationships with their children improved their satisfaction with life in general.[70]

Unless you are receiving alimony or child support from an ex-spouse, you are probably the sole source of support for your child, and that can create stress. You and your youngster may be living on less money than when you were married and will need to do some belt-tightening. Some working mothers volunteer to work overtime at their jobs, or take on a second part-time job in order to make ends meet. Until you find a job that can provide some financial security, economics can

---

[69] http://www.pewsocialtrends.org/2013/07/02/the-rise-of-single-fathers/

[70] http://blackfathers.org/2011/09/single-black-fathers-little-known-facts-revealed/

be the overriding concern in your life. This means that your school-age child may see less of you and have less money to buy things he was accustomed to having. That can stress your relationship with him and can add to his resentment of you for getting divorced. Make sure he understands your economic realities and that you need to work more than you would like. Reassure him that even when you are away from him, you think about him. A routine after-school phone call to him from work may ease the distance he feels between you.[71]

A single parent's responsibilities certainly do not stop the moment work ends each day. You may have what seems like a full day's worth of tasks awaiting you at home from cooking dinner to doing laundry to helping your child with homework. Although these same obligations are faced by working mothers who are married, a single parent has to face these responsibilities alone, without the helping hand of a husband. For that reason, many single parents feel chronically fatigued. They often feel physically and emotionally exhausted and find themselves yelling more at their children. As their youngsters move through middle childhood and normally become more opinionated and challenging of their parents' points of view, more arguments may develop.[72]

Unless single parents set aside some down time to rest and recuperate, they can experience burnout and depression, feeling hopeless and helpless about trying to transform their lives into something more manageable. Having a little emotional support or help around the house from another adult can go a long way toward helping you to cope.[73]

---

[71] http://www.healthychildren.org/English/family-life/family-dynamics/types-of-families/Pages/The-Challenges-of-Single-Parenthood.aspx

[72] http://www.healthychildren.org/English/family-life/family-dynamics/types-of-families/Pages/The-Challenges-of-Single-Parenthood.aspx

[73] http://www.healthychildren.org/English/family-life/family-dynamics/types-of-families/Pages/The-Challenges-of-Single-Parenthood.aspx

Single parents often feel they have no time for themselves, whether it is to exercise at the gym or to have dinner with friends. Even if they can find time for these individual pursuits, they may be so tired that they have no energy for them. Being deprived of sleep will take a toll on anyone, parent or child. Sometimes the best that you can do for yourself and your child is to get more sleep each night. For some single parents, during or after the divorce, their lack of energy is dramatic and part of a more serious depression. Persistent sadness, irritability, difficulty sleeping, and weight gain or loss are all signs of depression. A depressed parent has much less to offer a child. If you are depressed, speak to your physician or a mental-health professional.[74]

A child's difficult behavior in the aftermath of his parents' separation tends to be temporary and will probably diminish as the crisis of divorce subsides. However, there are a number of troublesome behavioral patterns that, if persistent, are signs of more serious problems. Boys and girls in middle childhood often respond differently in these situations as they adjust to living in a single-parent household. For example, boys may become very aggressive after their father moves out, making it difficult for their mother to assert her authority.[75]

In this situation, mothers need to work hard to maintain their authority as soon as this behavior becomes apparent, or matters could get out of control as the child's aggressiveness escalates. At the same time, fathers need to be informed of the child's misbehavior and should support the ex-spouse's position as an authority figure. A phone call or a face-to-face conversation can often be part of this process. Fathers, however, should not be called in to rescue their ex-wives, since this will tend to undermine the mother's authority position

---

[74] http://www.healthychildren.org/English/family-life/family-dynamics/types-of-families/Pages/The-Challenges-of-Single-Parenthood.aspx

[75] Ibid

and could even cause additional misbehavior by the child as a way of forcing more contact with his father.[76]

Occasionally, boys will develop some of the departed father's behavior and assume a husband-like relationship with the mother. They may begin to comment on the mother's appearance, try to offer financial advice, become jealous if she starts to date, and otherwise attempt to assume an adult role in the family. Girls, by contrast, tend to become more reserved and withdrawn as their response to the changing family structure. They also sometimes assume a maternal role in relation to their mother and siblings. An eleven or twelve-year-old girl may have to run the household while her mother is working, which can rob her of her childhood and undoubtedly lead to an unhealthy relationship between her and her siblings. If the girl is living with her father, she might also develop some of the departed mother's behavior and function as a "wife" to her father. These are not healthy patterns.[77]

We all have challenges in our lives; however, single mothers have some huge battles to overcome. That is not to say that the cross they carry is larger than the one that each of us has to carry. The fact is, single mothers do find themselves left alone to deal with financial strain, social isolation, decision pressure, guilt, and fatigue; all problems with available solutions, as shown in Table 4, Five Toughest Single Mom Struggles.

[76] http://www.healthychildren.org/English/family-life/family-dynamics/types-of-families/Pages/The-Challenges-of-Single-Parenthood.aspx

[77] Ibid

TABLE 4 FIVE TOUGHEST SINGLE MOM STRUGGLES[78]

Number	Struggles	Solution
1	**Financial strain**: The most common life events that lead to single parenthood — death, divorce, etc. — upset more than just a mother's marital status. They upset her financial balance, and leave one adult shouldering a load that is typically carried by two.	While one cannot control others (like an ex-spouse), one can control her decisions and get organized and intentional about how they handle their money to lessen the stress. They can consult with a financial planner, or take a course at church like Dave Ramsey's Financial Peace University to help make every dollar go as far as possible. What children need most, we have in abundance: love. Lavish them with love, and lay down the guilt of not being able to give them every material thing they desire.
2	**Social isolation**: Single moms sometimes feel trapped underneath a mountain of responsibility that never allows them to invest in friendships, much less find another companion for life. Working single moms say the guilt of leaving their kids in the evening to do something just for them is crushing. Add to that the cost of hiring a sitter and getting out of the house for adult interaction seems almost impossible.	Single moms need friendships and encouragement. Look for environments that allow for some social time while keeping the kids occupied or entertained: a church small group that offers childcare, an exercise class at a gym with a kids' space, or a play date with other parents. Once a month, splurge for that sitter or trade out childcare with another parent to go to dinner with friends and talk about what is going on in your life.

---

[78] http://www.imom.com/mom-life/
encouragement/5-toughest-single-mom-struggles/

Number	Struggles	Solution
3	**Decision pressure**: Parenting is hard. There are many gray areas and the game changes daily as children grow. For married parents, there is at least another adult to talk to, and to share the burden of making tough decisions. Single parents bear the weight of all of those tough calls — where to go to school, which friends are okay, or when a child is mature enough for a new privilege or responsibility — alone. The emotional burden can wear a mom down in a hurry.	Seek out a trusted parenting mentor or peer to bounce off some thoughts. It might be a friend from church, parents, or a pastor or counselor. Make sure that the people who are chosen share the same fundamental values. Although the final parenting decision will still be the single mom's to make, getting some feedback on a parental plan can lessen the anxiety and embolden her to do the hard things that parenting sometimes requires.
4	**Guilt**. Is there any end to the guilt a single parent feels? If a mother knows that her decisions contributed to the current family status, it is especially present. There is guilt about the financial things one cannot provide, guilt about the time spent away from kids, guilt about the things one just cannot do because of her situation. Regardless of how children became the kids of a single parent, a single mother worries daily about the effect that it is having on them and feels responsible.	Own your mistakes, learn from them and move on. We all make mistakes, and the guilt we feel is only helpful inasmuch as it helps us to correct problems and become better people. If your current situation is the result of the mistakes of another, do yourself a favor and forgive. The burden of anger is too much for you to bear forever. You cannot get in a time machine and fix the past, but you can do your best to make today better, so focus your energy there. Work on relationships with your kids' other parent/stepparent so that they feel less friction. Be a great example today and trust God to fill in the gaps that are beyond your reach.

Number	Struggles	Solution
5	**Fatigue**. Single moms are doing alone what was designed to be a two-person job. The fact that a single mom often feels physically, emotionally, and spiritually worn out is not just her imagination. However, because her kids depend on her, she cannot afford to push herself past a certain point. Single moms must take care of themselves and their health in order to be there for their children.	Find ways to take a breather, even if you have to swap out childcare with another single parent to make it happen. Spend that time recharging in some way that will continue to pay benefits when the busyness kicks back in: with exercise, spiritual growth, or good old-fashioned sleep. Look at these quick and easy energy boosters for ideas! It is not selfish to maintain the engine that keeps your home running: you.

6. CHAINS AND STRUGGLES OF A CHECKERED PAST

As African-Americans, we have had our battles in this world spiritually, socially, mentally, physically, and economically. However, the mental and economic battles have kept African-Americans in chains. They are struggles from the past that have continually kept the minds of African-Americans enslaved to those things that are in the past. We are a race that has become so concerned with ourselves that we have allowed the enemy to put us into a deep spiritual sleep. For unbelievers, the sleep is a spiritual death from which they need to be awakened and allow Jesus to be Lord of their lives. For believers, the sleep is a spiritual deadness in which they find themselves with a religion and no relationship with Jesus. The result is a failure to be led by the Holy Spirit. The bottom line is that both believers and unbelievers have the choice of being mentally and economically free from their past struggles. Does this mean the struggles of racism and its checkered past are now a thing of the past for blacks? Not exactly!

Today's brand of racism is not easily seen. Even the most loving white people do not want to admit it exists. Even more perplexing, many black men and women move up and blend into the mainstream of white society. Upper-class blacks work hard to blend in well. This also helps to create the illusion that no racial problem exists in America. As a result, those who would rather deny that racism exists find plenty of evidence of its demise. On the other hand, those who feel the pinch of it find plenty of evidence that it is still alive and well. In spite of all our well-intentional laws, in spite of a constitution that says all men are created equal, in spite of an abundance of good white people all over this world, in spite of all of these things, the death of racism has not yet come. Racism lives because of the insecurity of man and the inability of a man to love his fellow man, regardless of color, race or creed.[79]

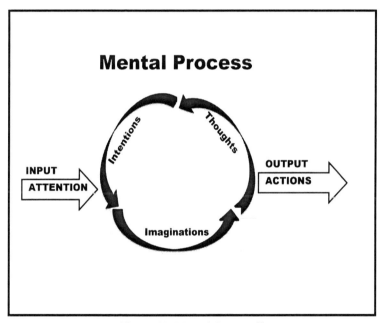

Figure 11. Mental Process.[80]

---

[79] Asher Ledwidge. *Saving the Black Culture A Revolution of Hope-Black Unity-Brotherly Love*. (Clermont, Florida: Self-published Asher Ledwidge; 2004),12-13.

[80] Dr. Winfred Verreen. Elim Baptist Ministries

It was a strong spiritual relationship with God that gave blacks the strength and wisdom to overcome slavery and racism. It is going to take a stronger relationship today to overcome the past hurts that have our undivided attention. As African-Americans, we have to confess that we have control over our intentions, thoughts, and imaginations. They are elements of our mental process. Our mental process, Figure 11, shows that what we give our attention to will determine our actions. We control what we allow to enter into our minds, and we control what leaves our minds. If we continue to dwell on all the negative things that have happened and can happen, we leave very little energy and time to think and meditate on all of the positive things that have happened to reshape our thoughts, change our intentions, and positively feed our imaginations.

If we are not prayerful, we will continue to find ourselves digressing instead of progressing. I do not mean as individuals; I mean as a race. Individually, we have found degrees of freedom and success, according to man's definition, but not according to God's definition. Success, according to man, is defined in the things we have and the things that we have accomplished. However, when we look at things from a biblical perspective, we realize that everything we see is temporal and it will pass away. That fact can be confirmed in 2 Corinthians 4:18, "While we look not at the things which are seen, but at the things which are not seen: for the things which are seen are temporal, but the things which are not seen are eternal."

There is no question about it; blacks have a very checkered past, one that can bring pain or bring victory. The choice is up to individuals to make. The question is: What do we want to focus on as we move into the future? If we focus on the past and what we see in the natural, we will continue to find ourselves stuck in bondage. If we focus on God and His Kingdom, we will find freedom and forgiveness. It is beneficial to study the past; however, we should not park in the past. In other words, learn from the past and move on to the present. Yes, slavery for blacks has a long history, but we can use history to learn how to move forward.

Beginning in Virginia in 1619, slavery served as the impetus for racial, economic inequities. It prohibited blacks from being paid for their labor while simultaneously creating vast amounts of wealth for its profiteers. Despite the majority of whites who did not own slaves, the social, political and economic gains achieved through this system were distributed to benefit only whites (and their descendants). This division of wealth served as the foundation for the economic divide between whites and blacks.[81]

In 1863, after Lincoln passed the Emancipation Proclamation, blacks were far from being perceived as equal. In fact, in order to bind the nation's wounds from the Civil War and promote national unity, whites were conferred privileged status, and blacks' social, political and economic interests were sacrificed. Racist and segregationist policies, most notably Jim Crow, were instituted to maintain the trajectory of African-Americans' exclusion from economic opportunities. Through Jim Crow, the best jobs, neighborhoods, schools and hospitals were reserved for whites; relegating African-Americans to impoverished conditions, only further widening economic inequities (e.g., unemployment, poverty, etc.) over generations.[82]

In addition to vast unemployment and poverty, millions of African-Americans were also falsely imprisoned and sold as laborers. From the end of Reconstruction until WWI, falsely imprisoned blacks were leased to small-town entrepreneurs, provincial farmers, and corporations looking for abundant, cheap labor. In addition, fear, intimidation and

---

[81] http://blackamericaweb.com/2013/02/06/
the-history-of-racial-economic-inequality-part-1-slavery/

[82] http://blackamericaweb.com/2013/02/06/
the-history-of-racial-economic-inequality-part-1-slavery/.

even death (ownership was one of the primary causes for lynching) were employed against blacks for attempting to secure any socioeconomic mobility for themselves and their families. This country was evolving into a world-class economic superpower from the capital generated from slavery and Jim Crow policies and any accumulation of wealth by blacks that decreased the labor force would not be tolerated.[83]

For decades to follow, African-Americans continued to be excluded from wealth and opportunity, and their exclusion would only continue with the administration of the New Deal, the greatest expansion of the American middle class in history.[84]

Blacks throughout history have been just as guilty of keeping blacks from advancing as whites. Several times in my professional career, opportunities for promotion were available for me to advance and in each case it was sabotaged by a black man. After each incident, I personally confronted the individual with documented facts of what they had done and in each case, it was denied. It was an example of blacks enjoying their high positions as minorities in corporate America with no desire to share that position of success with other blacks.

Our country has made tremendous progress, which is evident with the inauguration of President Barack Obama into his second term. However, the racial wounds and vestiges of centuries of institutional racism and economic oppression remain. In 1865, just after the Emancipation, African-Americans owned .05% of the nation's wealth; by 1990, African-Americans only owned 1% percent. If wealth is an indicator by which we measure a person, a family, and the community's economic security, then this stark disparity in wealth gives us insight into why African-American communities continue to struggle.[85]

---

[83] Ibid.

[84] Ibid.

[85] http://blackamericaweb.com/2013/02/06/
the-history-of-racial-economic-inequality-part-1-slavery/

We cannot achieve economic parity until we work to advance policy that explicitly includes African-Americans and tackles the centuries of racial, economic exclusion. "Django Unchained" and "Lincoln" have opened the door to having a thoughtful and honest conversation around slavery. Now we must keep that door open, acknowledge slavery's economic impacts and discuss real solutions to closing the racial, economic divide.[86]

Unfortunately, blacks are holding un-forgiveness that dates back as far as two hundred years. When I open my Bible, I see scriptures that clearly tell me that God requires us to forgive others and that un-forgiveness is still a sin. Matthew 6:14-15, "For if you forgive men their trespasses, your heavenly Father will also forgive you. |15| But if you don't forgive men their trespasses, neither will your Father forgive your trespasses."

Since the majority of African-Americans today (83%) confess to being Christians, it should not be a news flash that Jesus is returning for a Church that does not have spots, wrinkles, or blemishes. Nevertheless, through our un-forgiveness African-Americans are not exempt from Ephesians 5:27, "That he might present it to himself a glorious church, not having spot, or wrinkle, or any such thing; but that it should be holy and without blemish." If we want to be included in the glorious church, we need to stop living with selfishness, un-forgiveness, cliques, sin, ungodliness, and no respect for authority. In addition, we need to release the pain and wounds inflicted from a checkered past into the hands of the Lord. It is time for us to wake up and be what God has called us to be, do what the Holy Spirit speaks to our spirits to do, and live as children of the King of Kings under the authority of a God who loves us all, unconditionally.

---

[86] Ibid.

According to the U.S. Religious Landscape Survey, conducted in 2007 by the Pew Research Center's Forum on Religion & Public Life, Black Americans, "are markedly more religious on a variety of measures than the U.S. population as a whole." It cited that 87% of Blacks (vs. 83% of all Americans) are affiliated with a religion. It also found that 79 % of Blacks (vs. 56% overall) say that religion is "very important in their life" as shown in Figure 12.

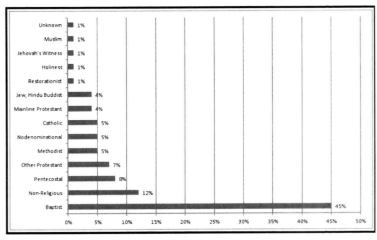

Figure 12. Black Americans religion.

Many scholars estimate that 15-30% of Africans imported as slaves were Muslim. The majority of the remaining practiced indigenous forms of worship. All were converted to Christianity. Most became Baptist, although slaves from Louisiana became Catholic because of the French settlers in that area. Today 83% of African-Americans are Christian, and only 1% identifies themselves as Muslim.[88]

---

[87] http://blackdemographics.com/culture/religion/

[88] http://blackdemographics.com/culture/religion/

From this statistical perspective, it has been noted that there has been a time in history that African-Americans, like the people in Ephesus, were awakened and committed to truth. History points to the fact that Blacks made it through some of the most difficult times in their lives by singing psalms, hymns, and spiritual songs to the Lord. This is a good time to note that repeating history is not always a bad thing. In fact, sometimes history should be repeated when it is in our best interest. According to Ephesians 5, we should sing Psalms and hymns. It is a step in the right direction, a step towards the Kingdom and presence of God.

Ephesians 5:14-21
Wherefore he saith, Awake thou that sleepest, and arise from the dead, and Christ shall give thee light. [15] See then that ye walk circumspectly, not as fools, but as wise, [16] Redeeming the time, because the days are evil. [17] Wherefore be ye not unwise, but understanding what the will of the Lord is. [18] And be not drunk with wine, wherein is excess; but be filled with the Spirit; [19] Speaking to yourselves in psalms and hymns and spiritual songs, singing and making melody in your heart to the Lord; [20] Giving thanks always for all things unto God and the Father in the name of our Lord Jesus Christ; [21] Submitting yourselves one to another in the fear of God.

Unfortunately, today, we sing Psalms and hymns in segregated places of worship. What is disturbing is that it exists in the one place where people should be color-blind and full of love and forgiveness, a place where people should be setting the standard and being an example for the world to see unconditional love. That place is the church. The one day we set aside to worship and serve the true and living God is the one day we stand divided into many of our communities because of the color of our skin. Nevertheless, the majority of churches continue to preach and teach being one body in Christ according to the Word of God as we continue to be a body that is broken and torn apart by our differences.

1 Corinthians 12:12-14
For as the body is one, and hath many members, and all the members of that one body, being many, are one body: so also is Christ. [13] For by one Spirit are we all baptized into one body, whether we be Jews or Gentiles, whether we be bond or free; and have been all made to drink into one Spirit. [14] For the body is not one member, but many.

One of the major misconceptions that has been made in our society is for people to believe that they are better than others. Thankfully, in the eyes of God we are all on the same level. Not one of us — regardless of our race, nationality, education, or success — is better than anyone else. Understanding and accepting this fact would eliminate all aspects of racism and biased attitudes towards others. Figure 13 shows a visual of God's position compared to a man. God is not in a box, and He cannot be contained.

Oh, how great it will be when we open our eyes and hearts and begin to live what we preach and teach. How beautiful it would be to see one another as Christ sees us. Before that can happen, we need to do several things: we need to press past what we see in the physical, let the past go, and stand on the Word of God. Ephesians 3:20-21, "Now unto him that is able to do exceeding abundantly above all that we ask or think, according to the power that worketh in us, [21] Unto him be glory in the church by Christ Jesus throughout all ages, world without end. Amen." We serve a God who can do more than we can imagine or think. It is up to us to believe and trust Him to do exceeding abundantly, above all

Figure 13. God and man.

that we ask or think. That is remarkable because there is no end to our asking.

God's Word in Ephesians 4:23 says, "And be renewed in the spirit of your mind." The mind is a part of the soul and came in the created body when God blew the breath of life in the created man. We need to guard our minds against some of the things we think about on a daily basis that are not spiritually beneficial to anyone. We need to begin to think like the scriptures tell us in Philippians 4:8, "Finally, brethren, whatsoever things are true, whatsoever things are honest, whatsoever things are just, whatsoever things are pure, whatsoever things are lovely, whatsoever things are of good report; if there be any virtue, and if there be any praise, think on these things." It sounds easy to do, but it is not, because we have been conditioned to see and think about the negative more than the positive. Think about it. How often do news stations report about the great things that happen in society? Not often. Why? Because bad news is more popular and profitable. However, that does not give anyone an excuse for not guarding his or her mind against a destructive past to move forward in life. Figure 14 shows how we all exercise reason with a free will to make choices in life. It is up to individuals to make the right choice in life or be prepared for the consequences.

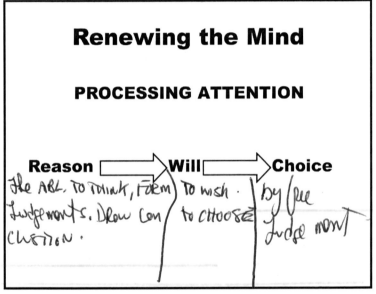

Renewing the Mind

PROCESSING ATTENTION

Reason ⟶ **Will** ⟶ **Choice**

The ABL. TO THINK, FORM Judgements, Draw Con clusion. *TO wish. to CHOOSE* *by free Judge ment*

Figure 14. Renewing the mind and processing attention.[89]

Scripture tells us in Romans 12:2, "And be not conformed to this world: but be ye transformed by the renewing of your mind, that ye may prove what is that good, and acceptable, and perfect, will of God." At some point between birth and death, we have to make a decision that has eternal implications. The correct decision is to not be conformed to this world. We walk in obedience to the Word of God by allowing

[89] Dr. Winfred Verreen, Elim Baptist Ministries

His Word to transform us and renew our minds, that we may have a relationship with the Lord and not a religious experience. When we have a relationship with the Lord, we can walk in the perfect will of God and show the love of Christ.

It is no hidden secret that whites have done many bad and evil things to African-Americans in the past. Many times, they were done at the expense of misquoting the Bible. In fact, we can go to the beginning of the Bible to see wickedness as early as Genesis 6:5, "And God saw that the wickedness of man was great in the earth and that every imagination of the thoughts of his heart was only evil continually." Nevertheless, the opportunity to read the Word and learn the truth is now available to all African-Americans who choose to break the chains of their past. Regardless of how bad or hopeless the situation may look, God is the creator of all things, and He is the head of the church.

Colossians 1:16-26
For by him were all things created, that are in heaven, and that are in earth, visible and invisible, whether they be thrones, or dominions, or principalities, or powers: all things were created by him, and for him:|17|And he is before all things, and by him all things consist. |18| And he is the head of the body, the church: who is the beginning, the first-born from the dead; that in all things he might have the preeminence. |19| For it pleased the Father that in him should all fulness dwell; |20| And, having made peace through the blood of his cross, by him to reconcile all things unto himself; by him, I say, whether they be things in earth, or things in heaven. |21| And you, that were sometime alienated and enemies in your mind by wicked works, yet now hath he reconciled |22| In the body of his flesh through death, to present you holy and unblameable and

unreproveable in his sight:[23] If ye continue in the faith grounded and settled, and be not moved away from the hope of the gospel, which ye have heard , and which was preached to every creature which is under heaven; whereof I Paul am made a minister; [24] Who now rejoice in my sufferings for you, and fill up that which is behind of the afflictions of Christ in my flesh for his body's sake, which is the church: [25] Whereof I am made a minister, according to the dispensation of God which is given to me for you, to fulfil the Word of God; [26] Even the mystery which hath been hid from ages and from generations, but now is made manifest to his saints:

The Word of God is full of scriptures, advice, direction, and examples that can set anyone free from their past. Hebrews 4:12, "For the Word of God is quick, and powerful, and sharper than any two-edged sword, piercing even to the dividing asunder of soul and spirit, and of the joints and marrow, and is a discerner of the thoughts and intents of the heart." One only has to take the time to read the Word and have faith to believe. Proverbs 23:7, "For as he thinketh in his heart, so is he: Eat and drink, saith he to thee; but his heart is not with thee." Yes, it begins with what one thinks of himself. However, it started when God breathed life in the natural man and he became a living soul, Figure 15.
Our faith in God is the key to everything. There are no exceptions, and there are no alternatives to having faith in God. When one has faith in God and the determination and will in their hearts to forgive, God has promised that we can have whatever we ask. Now, that is a promise worthy of praise!

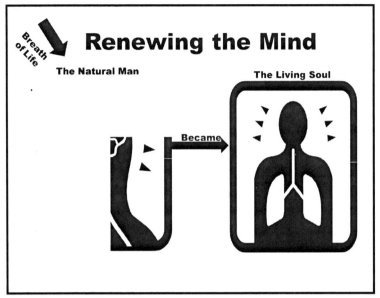

Figure 15. Renewing the mind, the living soul.[90]

Mark 11:22-26

And Jesus answering saith unto them, Have faith in God. [23] For verily I say unto you, That whosoever shall say unto this mountain, Be thou removed , and be thou cast into the sea; and shall not doubt in his heart, but shall believe that those things which he saith shall come to pass; he shall have whatsoever he saith . [24]Therefore I say unto you, What things soever ye desire, when ye pray, believe that ye receive them, and ye shall have them. [25] And when ye stand praying, forgive , if ye have ought against any: that your Father also which is in heaven may forgive you your trespasses. [26] But if ye do not forgive, nei- ther will your Father which is in heaven forgive your trespasses.

---

[90] Dr. Winfred Verreen, Elim Baptist Ministries

When there is no faith in God, there are limitations to reasoning: As human beings, we use our created abilities to process information. We have limited ability to decipher all the information in our minds to make sound decisions, although we are left to choose and make decisions on our accord. However, we can allow divine intervention in our reasoning, in accordance with Proverbs 3: 5-6, "Trust in the Lord with all thine heart; and lean not unto thine own understanding. [6] In all thy ways acknowledge him, and he shall direct thy paths." We do not have to depend on information that restricts us to our human limitations when we have a God we can trust to deliver, heal, and restore.

African-Americans have made the mistake too often of trusting man and seeking ungodly counsel, only to walk away not hating just an individual, but hating an entire race. The lies encountered from one individual should never justify hating an entire race. Hate can be corrected by seeking Godly counseling, according to the Word of God.

Psalm 1:1-6
Blessed is the man that walketh not in the counsel of the ungodly, nor standeth in the way of sinners, nor sitteth in the seat of the scornful. [2] But his delight is in the law of the Lord; and in his law doth he meditate day and night. [3] And he shall be like a tree planted by the rivers of water, that bringeth forth his fruit in his season; his leaf also shall not wither; and whatsoever he doeth shall prosper. [4] The ungodly are not so: but are like the chaff which the wind driveth away. [5] Therefore the ungodly shall not stand in the judgment, nor sinners in the congregation of the righteous. [6] For the Lord knoweth the way of the righteous: but the way of the ungodly shall perish.

The scriptures are clear. We are not to seek or receive counsel from a world of ungodly counselors. When we do, we risk losing the blessing of God. God's desire to bless us has nothing to do with our race or past struggles. 3 John 1:2, "Beloved, I wish above all things that thou mayest prosper and be in health, even as thy soul prospereth." Now, if God wishes that we would prosper and be in good health, should we be concerned about what a man thinks, says, or does? Of course not!

On the other hand, springing from the heart are the mental and moral attributes of man and the seat of consciousness, influencing our thought process. This includes both the rational and emotional elements, governed by a wicked heart as depicted in Figure 16, reflecting the connections of the mind and spirit from the heart of a natural man who is not a believer of Christ.

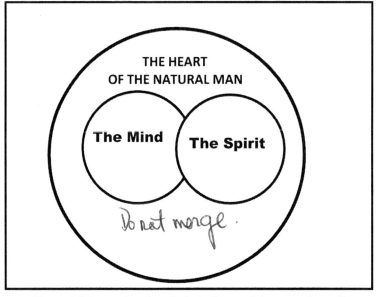

Figure 16. Renewing the mind, the heart of the natural man.[91]

In contrast, springing from the heart of a spirit-filled man are the mental and moral attributes of man and the seat of consciousness, influencing our thought process. This included both the rational and emotional elements, governed by a new heart and the presence of the Holy Spirit. Reflecting the connections of the mind and spirit from the heart of a man who is a believer of Christ is depicted in Figure 17.

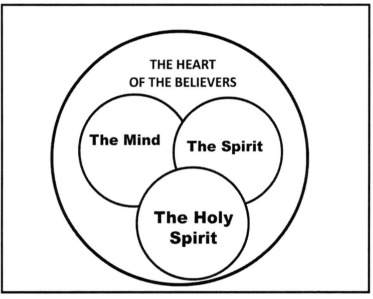

Figure 17. Renewing the mind, the heart of the believers.[92]

It is easier to release our struggles when we have Christ in our lives; all we have to do is trust in a caring God and ask the Holy Spirit to illuminate our darkness. The obstacle for most of us is that our egos fool us into thinking we can solve all our problems with the right books, professionals, tools, or skills. We seriously believe that we would be happier and our children better if only we had more money, more time, fewer

---

[92] Dr. Winfred Verreen, Elim Baptist Ministries

hassles or a better past. It seems to take forever for African-Americans to accept the fact that we cannot fix everything. Furthermore, we do not have to fix everything. We can leave things God has asked us to leave in His hands in the hands of God. When we finally catch on to this truth, things will go more smoothly for our children and us. With God, there is a way out of every challenge and a path into God's blessings. We should embrace every opportunity to let God move in and through us. If we make connecting with our inner wisdom a comfortable habit, consulting with the Divine Parent on a regular basis, we will find that our stress level goes down and our parent comfort level goes up. Children come equipped with spiritual tools and internal spiritual power. The most helpful thing we can do is to remind them of that connection and those tools when problems arise.[93]

---

[93] Mimi Doe and Marsha Walch. *10 Principles for Spiritual Parenting*. (New York, NY: Harper Collins Publishers, Inc.; 1998), 298.

7. THE FUTURE OF THE AFRICAN-AMERICAN YOUTH

The majority of black teens, at some point in life, have faced or will face racial discrimination. These experiences are associated with an increased risk of mental health problems, according to a new study. "Sixty years after Brown vs. Board of Education, racism remains a toxic stressor commonly experienced by youth of color," said Lee M. Pachter, D.O., a professor of pediatrics at Drexel University College of Medicine and Chief of General Pediatrics at St. Christopher's Hospital for Children in Philadelphia.[94]

"Consequently, these experiences are encountered during adolescence; a critically sensitive period for identity development is of great concern, as is our finding of slightly higher rates of depression, anxiety, and social phobias in those youth who have more experiences with discrimination." For the study, which was presented at the Pediatric Academic Societies' (PAS) annual meeting in Vancouver, British Columbia, Canada, the researchers analyzed data from the National Survey of American Life, which examines

---

[94] http://psychcentral.com/news/2014/05/04/discrimination-contributes-to-mental-health-woes-in-black-teens/69337.html

racial, ethnic, and cultural influences on the mental health of African-Americans and Afro-Caribbeans. [95]

Interviews were conducted with a nationally representative sample of 1,170 adolescents between the ages of 13 and 17. The study looked at the experiences of black youth of Caribbean ancestry and ethnicity separate from African-American youth; Pachter pointed out. "Because of differences in culture, pre and post-immigration experiences, and other factors, it is important to differentiate groups that generally are lumped together as 'black' in the same way that Latinos are separated into subgroups, such as Mexican-American, Puerto Rican, and Cuban," he noted.[96]

The survey found that 85 percent of adolescents experience racial discrimination. During their lifetime, six percent experienced major depression; 17 percent suffered from anxiety while 13 percent had social phobia. In the year before they were surveyed, four percent of teens had major depression, and 14 percent experienced anxiety, the researcher reported. More experiences with discrimination were associated with a higher likelihood of major depression, anxiety disorder and social phobia during one's lifetime, according to the study's findings. These associations were present for both African-Americans and Afro-Caribbeans, for males and females, and for younger and older teens, the study found.[97]

Results also showed that increasing levels of racial discrimination had a greater effect on Afro-Caribbean youth, which experienced higher rates of anxiety than African-American teens, the researcher noted. "The challenge now is to identify interventions at the individual, family and community levels to lessen the mental health effects of racial

---

[95] Ibid.

[96] http://psychcentral.com/news/2014/05/04/discrimination-contributes-to-mental-health-woes-in-black-teens/69337.html.

[97] Ibid.

discrimination while we as a society grapple with ways to eliminate it as a toxic stressor," Pachter concluded.[98]

At the same time, as African-Americans, it is imperative for parents and successful blacks to equip our black youth for success. After all, successful people give thanks and praises to mentors, family, friends, and productive people in their lives for their success, wealth, and helping them get through some very tough times. This author believes that point of view is correct because it is impossible to climb the ladder of success or accomplish anything in life by ourselves. However, let us put this in a biblical perspective; we cannot do anything without Christ. We live in a world that was created by God; everything that we see and touch belongs to Him. We own nothing in this world, and we will take nothing out of this world. We will leave this world the same way we entered, naked. Job 1:21, "And said, naked came I out of my mother's womb, and naked shall I return thither: the Lord gave, and the Lord hath taken away; blessed be the name of the Lord."

What we fail to realize is that we are only stewards of everything we have in our possession. It does not belong to us. It all belongs to God. In fact, we are not our own; we were bought with a price, a price that we can never repay or duplicate. That price was the blood of Jesus. 1 Corinthians 6:20, "For ye are bought with a price: therefore glorify God in your body, and in your spirit, which are God's."

Therefore, the world is right to believe we need mentors and influential people in our lives to make it in this world. Our young people are not excluded. The problem is the world is looking to the wrong mentors. The world is looking to man before looking to God. Trust me, man will fail us; sometimes intentionally, sometimes unintentionally, sometimes out of jealousy, sometimes out of anger, sometimes for personal gain, and sometimes just to cause pain. Nevertheless,

---

[98] Ibid.

regardless of the reason, failure is failure and pain is pain, and it is not easy for young black people to overcome these things alone.

Our young black boys and girls need mentors and people who love them in their own circles. They need mentors that have a committed relationship with the Lord, who not only know the Word of God, but also live and breathe God's word every day of their lives. However, there is a risk with having man as a mentor. The risk is that not everyone wants to see others become more successful than they have been; that is particularly true in the black community. Many blacks have experienced what is referred to as "crab mentality" many times in their lives. Crab mentality is a state of mind triggered by a spirit of jealousy, in which people climb on top of one another in an attempt to stop another from advancing.

It is very unfortunate that this type of behavior has been occurring for hundreds of years, and the black race is no exception. Some people are just evil and want to see others suffer when they suffer. A prime example of this type of mentality is reflected by the woman who lost her child in 1 Kings 3 and was willing to see an innocent baby die, just because she had lost her child:

1Kings 3:16-28
Then came there two women, that were harlots, unto the king, and stood before him. |17| And the one woman said, O my lord, I and this woman dwell in one house; and I was delivered of a child with her in the house. |18| And it came to pass the third day after that I was delivered, that this woman was delivered also: and we were together; there was no stranger with us in the house, save we two in the house. |19| And this woman's child died in the night; because she overlaid it. |20| And she arose at midnight, and took my son from beside me, while thine handmaid slept, and laid it in

her bosom, and laid her dead child in my bosom. [21] And when I rose in the morning to give my child suck, behold, it was dead: but when I had considered it in the morning, behold, it was not my son, which I did bear. [22] And the other woman said, Nay; but the living is my son, and the dead is thy son. And this said, No; but the dead is thy son, and the living is my son. Thus they spake before the king.[23] Then said the king, The one saith, This is my son that liveth, and thy son is the dead : and the other saith , Nay; but thy son is the dead , and my son is the living.[24] And the king said, Bring me a sword. And they brought a sword before the king. [25] And the king said, Divide the living child in two, and give half to the one, and half to the other. [26] Then spake the woman whose the living child was unto the king, for her bowels yearned upon her son, and she said, O my lord, give her the living child, and in no wise slay it. But the other said, Let it be neither mine nor thine, but divide it. [27] Then the king answered and said, Give her the living child, and in no wise slay it: she is the mother thereof. [28] And all Israel heard of the judgment which the king had judged; and they feared the king: for they saw that the wisdom of God was in him, to do judgment.

Nevertheless, when we have a Father who promises us that we will be blessed when we believe in Him, there is no reason or excuse to ever be jealous of the blessings of others. Jesus expects the best from us, and for us to be able to do "greater works." We should expect the same from one another as brothers and sisters in the Lord.

John 14:12-18
Verily, verily, I say unto you, He that believeth on me, the works that I do shall he do also; and greater

works than these shall he do; because I go unto my Father. |13| And whatsoever ye shall ask in my name, that will I do, that the Father may be glorified in the Son. |14| If ye shall ask any thing in my name, I will do it. |15| If ye love me, keep my commandments. |16| And I will pray the Father, and he shall give you another Comforter, that he may abide with you for ever; |17| Even the Spirit of truth; whom the world cannot receive, because it seeth him not, neither knoweth him: but ye know him; for he dwelleth with you, and shall be in you. |18| I will not leave you comfortless: I will come to you.

As Christians, we have to teach our young black boys and girls that we have a trio of mentors — the Father, the Son, and the Holy Ghost — that rejoice with every successful step we take. They are three very important people that we can boast about: God, Jesus and the Holy Spirit. If we do not share this good news with this generation, how can we expect to see changes?

There is one God; infinite, eternal, almighty, and perfect in holiness, truth, and love. In the unity of the godhead, there are three persons: Father, Son and Holy Spirit. They co-existent, they are co-equal, and they are co-eternal. The Father is not the Son, and the Son is not the Holy Spirit, yet each is truly Deity. One God: Father, Son and Holy Spirit, is the foundation of Christian faith and life.

God, the Father, is the Creator of heaven and earth. By His word and for His glory, He freely and supernaturally created the world from nothing. Through the same Word, He daily sustains all His creatures. He rules over all. He is Sovereign. His plans and purposes cannot be thwarted. He is faithful to every promise and works all things together for good to those who love Him. In His unfathomable grace, he gave His Son, Jesus Christ, for mankind's redemption.

Jesus Christ, the only begotten Son of God, was the eternal Word made flesh, supernaturally conceived by the Holy Spirit, born of the Virgin Mary. He was perfect in nature, teaching, and obedience. He is fully God and fully man. He was always with God and is God. Through Him, all things came into being and were created. He was before all things, and in Him all things hold together by the Word of his power. He is the image of the invisible God, the first-born of all creation, and in Him dwells the fullness of the godhead bodily. He is the only Savior for the sins of the world, having shed His blood and died a vicarious death on Calvary's cross. By His death in our place, He revealed divine love and upheld divine justice, removing our guilt and reconciling us to God. Having redeemed us from sin, the third day He rose bodily from the grave, victorious over death and the powers of darkness. He ascended into Heaven where He is at the right hand of God. He intercedes for his people and rules as Lord over all. He is the Head of His body, the Church, and should be adored, loved, served, and obeyed by all.

The Holy Spirit, the Lord and Giver of life, convicts the world of sin, righteousness, and judgment. Through the proclamation of the gospel, he persuades men to repent of their sins and confess Jesus as Lord. By the same Spirit, a person is led to trust in divine mercy. The Holy Spirit unites believers to Jesus Christ in faith, brings about the new birth and dwells within the regenerate. The Holy Spirit has come to glorify the Son, who in turn came to glorify the Father. He will lead the Church into a right understanding and rich application of the truth of God's Word. He is to be respected, honored, and worshiped as God, the Third Person of the Trinity. He is the only mentor worthy of praise and worship.

On the other hand, there are mentors who want to live their lives in us and through us. Unlike the people in this world, Christians receive their direction not from one source, but from unlimited sources and resources. Psalms 32:8 says,

"I will instruct thee and teach thee in the way which thou shalt go: I will guide thee with mine eye." No matter how successful the world is, we cannot trust them to lead us. Luke 6:39, "And he spake a parable unto them, Can the blind lead the blind? shall they not both fall into the ditch?" We have a God who has always known us, Jeremiah 1:5, "Before I formed thee in the belly I knew thee; and before thou camest forth out of the womb I sanctified thee, and I ordained thee a prophet unto the nations."

Be careful with mentors; they can become someone we look up to and admire based on their position, authority, and power. Take the safe route and follow Jesus.

1 Peter 2:21-25
For even hereunto were ye called: because Christ also suffered for us, leaving us an example, that ye should follow his steps: [22] Who did no sin, neither was guile found in his mouth: [23] Who, when he was reviled, reviled not again; when he suffered, he threatened not; but committed himself to him that judgeth righteously: [24] Who his own self bare our sins in his own body on the tree, that we, being dead to sins, should live unto righteousness: by whose stripes ye were healed. [25] For ye were as sheep going astray; but are now returned unto the Shepherd and Bishop of your souls

It is time for African-Americans to lead by example. Should we care about being a good example? Should we stop looking for someone else to be a good example for black youth? I can almost guarantee you that if we have been looking at others to be good examples for our race, we probably have been hurt and had to live through disappointments, let downs, confusion, and embarrassment.

No matter how successful or anointed man is, he is still a man, and he is not perfect. In fact, he is under constant attack by the enemy, just like you and I; and he is subject to losing some battles to the enemy on those days he takes his eyes off Christ and walks in the flesh.

• The danger in a man being a good example is we expect him to be perfect, without flaws, sin, or excuses. When a godly man sins, some of his followers lose interest in Christ and the Church. Men who were once admired for being leaders, Christians, and pastors have caused many young black youths to re-enter the world of sin after witnessing sins being committed by those they trusted. •

God never intended for us to take our eyes off Him and look to man; if a man were "all of that," Jesus would not have had to come down from Heaven. A true man of God will always point God's sheep to Jesus. When black youths are pointed to Jesus, they will be able to weather the storms of life. Jesus will have eyes on them 24 hours a day and seven days a week and He will never fail them.

It is hard to understand why many Christians would want people to look up to them as good examples and follow them when we know we do not have it all together. In fact, most of us in the church are viewed as insane because we do the same things Sunday after Sunday and look for different results; that, my brothers and sisters, is the definition of insanity.

If we are going to imitate something or someone, why not the Original? The Original Jesus was a sinless man. He never lied and was totally honest. When blamed, He did not answer back. When accused, He did not defend Himself. He was silent under all of the insults and false acquisitions. Can we follow His example? He suffered silently. Can we do these things? Has anyone ever thought that we were weak because we did not respond to his or her insults and lies? Probably not. Silence in the midst of lies, insults, and false accusations is strength in Christ. It is also the best example to display in front of young black youths.

Jesus trusted God, no matter how He was challenged. Do we? The answer is, "No." As African-Americans, the first thought that comes to our minds is revenge, a term often referred to in the black community as a "get back spirit." However, God's Word states that vengeance is the Lord's.

Romans 12:19-21:
Dearly beloved, avenge not yourselves, but rather give place unto wrath: for it is written, Vengeance is mine; I will repay, saith the Lord. [20] Therefore if thine enemy hunger, feed him; if he thirst, give him drink: for in so doing thou shalt heap coals of fire on his head. [21] Be not overcome of evil, but overcome evil with good.

Our young black children are often punished for behavior that they emulate from their parents. Black parents can no longer instruct their children to "do as I say and not as I do." If we cannot be a good example, we must point them to Jesus. If we are going to follow the example of Jesus, we can no longer be like lizards, easily blending in with the world to the point that people cannot tell the non-believers from the Christians. If we are going to be like a lizard, we should be blending in with Christ and the Word of God, leaving no doubt that we are children of God. Then, and only then, can we become difference makers; one who is willing to make sacrifices and put Christ first; not in words, but in everything we do to keep young black children on the right path.

Following the example that Jesus portrayed will never be easy. People will talk about us, and not everybody is going to like us. Therefore, the question is: "Do we care what people think and say about us?" Yes, for two reasons: 1.) Some things said could be true, and if it is true, we should humble ourselves and pray for change. 2.) It could be a lie. In that case, we can be specific in our prayers, so that we can forgive them and let it go. Nevertheless, when our African-American children witness these responses, they will make better choices and have better behavior.

Conversely, we are sitting back and allowing the government and non-Christian organizations to fix a spiritual problem. We need compassion to confront these issues. Compassion is not taught; it has to come from within the heart. When you have it, it drives you to unrest and moves you to action. I know African-Americans have compassion for our race because when a black person makes history by doing something extraordinary, we celebrate nationally by the thousands. Even more, when a white person commits a murder of a young black person, we hit the streets by the thousands in protest expressing our compassion for the loss of another black soul, following leaders who have not prayed or heard from God.

There will be no future for African-American youth if they cannot overcome poverty, poor education, and the incarceration of young black men. According to Hattery and Smith, around 50% of African-American children are poor because they are dependent on a single mother. In states like Wisconsin, in order for a child to be the recipient of welfare or receive the "bride fare," their parents must be married. Hattery acknowledges one truth about this law, which is that it recognizes that a child is entitled to the financial and emotional support of both parents. One of Hattery and Smith's solutions is founded around this idea. The government does require the noncustodial parents to pay a percentage to their child every month, but according to Hattery the only way this will help eliminate child poverty is if these policies are actively enforced.[99]

For the past 400 years of America's life, many African-Americans have been denied the proper education needed to

---

[99] http://en.m.wikipedia.org/wiki/African-American_family_structure

provide for the traditional American family structure. Hattery suggests that the schools and education resources available to most African-Americans are under-equipped and unable to provide their students with the knowledge needed to be college ready. In 2005, the Manhattan Institute for Policy Research report showed that even though integration has been pushed more recently, over the past 15 years there has been a 13% decline in integration in public schools. These same reports also show that in 2002, 56% of African-American students graduated from high school with a diploma, while 78% of white students graduated. If students do not feel they are learning, they will not continue to go to school. This conclusion is made from the Manhattan Institute for Policy Research report that stated only 23% of African-American students who graduated from public high school felt college ready. Hatterly suggests the government invest into the African-American family by investing in the African-American children's education. The solution is found in providing the same resources provided to schools that are predominantly white. According to Hatterly, through education equality the African-American family structure can increase the opportunity to prosper with equality in employment, wages, and health insurance.[100]

According to Hattery and Smith, 25-33% of African-American men are spending time in jail or prison. In comparison, Thomas, Krampe, and Newton state that 28% of African-American children do not live with any father representative. Furthermore, the government can stop the problems that many African-American children experience due to the absence of their father. Hatterly suggests probation or treatment for alcohol or drugs as alternatives to incarceration. Incarceration not only continues the negative assumption of the African-American family structure, but also

---

[100]http://en.m.wikipedia.org/wiki/African-American_family_structure

perpetuates poverty, single parenthood, and the separation of family units.[101]

These aspects proposed by Hatterly can work; however, this is my ideology. I recommend more parental involvement. I have witnessed African-American parents in my community who invest more in their cars and cell phones than their children's education. I have witnessed churches reaching out to under-privileged black children with tutoring programs where kids had to find a way to the church. Their parents could not be found on the premises. I have seen black parents argue about the price of a book or field trip, but not blink twice over the purchase of an expensive pair of tennis shoes or a designer purse.

It is all about priorities and choices. When African-Americans change their priorities and make better choices, their destinations will change. Living in debt with loans and credit cards is living in bondage. Proverbs 22:7, "The rich ruleth over the poor, and the borrower *is* servant to the lender." As African-Americans, we do not focus on net worth, but we focus on credit scores to receive better loans to buy things we do not need and cannot afford to impress people we do not know. We go into serious debt to purchase cars and homes to impress people who do not like us. What is worst is that we teach these bad habits and poor principles to our families. A good credit score means we have plenty of debts that we pay on time. When we save money and pay for the things we need, we do not need loans and credit cards. Putting our focus on needs versus wants results in better financial choices. Good stewardship (Table 5) and taking steps to climb out of debt (Table 6) will change our net worth. It changed my net worth, but most importantly, it changed my mindset from bondage thinking to freedom thinking with the help of God.

---

[101] http://en.m.wikipedia.org/wiki/African-American_family_structure

TABLE 5 GOOD STEWARDSHIP

No.	Answer the Following Questions Before Buying
1.	Is this a "want", "desire", or "need"?
2.	Have I prayed about it?
3.	Did God say yes?
4.	Can I do without it?
5.	Do I need it now? Can I wait for it?
6.	Will it cause problems if I buy it?
7.	Am I neglecting any needs to buy it?
8.	Will I worship it and not the Giver?
9.	Have I paid my tithes?
10.	Will I have an offering to give?
11.	Have I met all my financial obligations?
12.	Do I owe anyone money?

TABLE 6 STEPS TO CLIMBING OUT OF DEBT

No.	Steps to Climbing Out of Debt	Scripture
1.	Confess all sins and repent.	1 John 1:9
2.	Be humble.	1 Peter 5:6
3.	Pay tithes and offerings.	Malachi 3:8-11
4.	Create no new debts.	Proverbs 22:7
5.	Pay debts on time.	Ecclesiastes 5:9
6.	Stop seeking material things.	Luke 12:15
7.	Pray and wait on the Lord.	Philippians 4:6
8.	In everything, give thanks.	1 Thessalonians 5:18
9.	Be accountable to someone.	James 5:16
10.	Set goals to pay off bills (budget).	Psalms 37:21
11.	Seek the Kingdom of God.	Matthew 6:33
12.	Give! Give! Give! Give!	Luke 6:38

As a rule, we make time and sacrifices for the people and things we love. When the future of our children and our economic future become a priority, we will put all of the material lusts on hold and invest our finances, time, and energy into our African-American children's lives. When we do this, their choices will be better, thereby creating a better future in front of them.

8. CONFORMING TO A SINFUL WORLD

The world we live in today has drastically changed for the worst. Christian or non-Christian, the changes we have seen in recent years are disturbing and heartbreaking. We have lost our fear of God, have no desire to do the right thing, and the word "obedient" has become a foreign concept. We have lost our moral baseline; now everything is acceptable. If the majority wants it, the majority can have it.

Consequently, if it does not profit us, feel good to us, make us happy, excite us, or put us in a position to be recognized, we are not interested in doing what is morally correct. In fact, we do not consider what God wants or what God has called us to do. It is all about us. We even have the audacity to ask, "Where is God?" when He does not answer our prayers according to our timetable. When bad things happen to good people, we ask, "What kind of God would allow this to happen?" Nevertheless, we sit in silence as we witness a multitude of sins being birthed all around us out of a spirit of disobedience and selfishness.

As Christians, we are making a habit of conforming to this sinful world. We want all of the material things the world has, we fight for positions like the world, and we lie, steal, kill, and seek the pleasures of this world. All of this is totally against the Word of God according to Romans 12:2, "And be not conformed to this world: but be ye transformed by the renewing of your mind, that ye may prove what is that good, and acceptable, and perfect, will of God."

The fact is we can talk about all the things in this world that we do not like and continue to do nothing about it, or we can come to the conclusion that no matter what anyone else decides to do, we will do the right thing. We will walk in obedience. As individuals, we are always in a position to make good choices as was Jonah, but Jonah chose not to be obedient, despite being in a position where he could have positively affected the world.

The name Jonah means "dove" and Jonah was a sensitive and caring prophet. He was the son of Amittai, whose name means "my truth." So in Jonah we have a very caring prophet who was the son of truth who chose to walk in disobedience to God.

Jonah: 1:1-17
Now the word of the LORD came unto Jonah the son of Amittai, saying, [2] Arise, go to Nineveh, that great city, and cry against it; for their wickedness is come up before me. [3] But Jonah rose up to flee unto Tarshish from the presence of the LORD, and went down to Joppa; and he found a ship going to Tarshish: so he paid the fare thereof, and went down into it, to go with them unto Tarshish from the presence of the LORD. [4] But the LORD sent out a great wind into the sea, and there was a mighty tempest in the sea, so that the ship was like to be broken. [5] Then the mariners were afraid, and cried every man unto his god, and cast forth the wares that were in the ship into the sea, to lighten it of them. But Jonah was gone down into the sides of the ship; and he lay, and was fast asleep. [6] So the shipmaster came to him, and said unto him, What meanest thou, O sleeper?

arise, call upon thy God, if so be that God will think upon us, that we perish not. [7] And they said every one to his fellow, Come , and let us cast lots, that we may know for whose cause this evil is upon us. So they cast lots, and the lot fell upon Jonah. [8] Then said they unto him, Tell us, we pray thee, for whose cause this evil is upon us; What is thine occupation? and whence comest thou? what is thy country? and of what people art thou? [9] And he said unto them, I am an Hebrew; and I fear the LORD, the God of heaven, which hath made the sea and the dry land. [10] Then were the men exceedingly afraid, and said unto him, Why hast thou done this? For the men knew that he fled from the presence of the LORD, because he had told them. [11] Then said they unto him, What shall we do unto thee, that the sea may be calm unto us? for the sea wrought, and was tempestuous. [12] And he said unto them, Take me up, and cast me forth into the sea; so shall the sea be calm unto you: for I know that for my sake this great tempest is upon you. [13] Nevertheless the men rowed hard to bring it to the land; but they could not: for the sea wrought, and was tempestuous against them. [14] Wherefore they cried unto the LORD, and said, We beseech thee, O LORD, we beseech thee, let us not perish for this man's life, and lay not upon us innocent blood: for thou, O LORD, hast done as it pleased thee. [15] So they took up Jonah, and cast him forth into the sea: and the sea ceased from her raging. [16] Then the men feared the LORD exceedingly, and offered a sacrifice unto the LORD, and made vows. [17] Now the LORD had prepared a great fish to swallow up Jonah. And Jonah was in the belly of the fish three days and three nights.

Subsequently, disobedience and sin brings storms and tempests into our souls, families, churches, and nations. However, the good news is we can always cry out to God with a repentant heart for his grace and mercy, unlike Ananias and Sapphira who were not under the dispensation of God's grace in Acts 5.

Acts 5:1-11

But a certain man named Ananias, with Sapphira his wife, sold a possession, [2] And kept back part of the price, his wife also being privy to it, and brought a certain part, and laid it at the apostles' feet. [3] But Peter said, Ananias, why hath Satan filled thine heart to lie to the Holy Ghost, and to keep back part of the price of the land? [4] Whiles it remained, was it not thine own? and after it was sold, was it not in thine own power? why hast thou conceived this thing in thine heart? thou hast not lied unto men, but unto God. [5] And Ananias hearing these words fell down, and gave up the ghost: and great fear came on all them that heard these things. [6] And the young men arose, wound him up, and carried him out, and buried him. [7] And it was about the space of three hours after, when his wife, not knowing what was done, came in. [8] And Peter answered unto her, Tell me whether ye sold the land for so much? And she said, Yea, for so much. [9] Then Peter said unto her, How is it that ye have agreed together to tempt the Spirit of the Lord? behold, the feet of them which have buried thy husband are at the door, and shall carry thee out. [10] Then fell she down straightway at his feet, and yielded up the ghost: and the young men came in, and found her dead, and, carrying her forth, buried her by her husband. [11] And great fear came upon all the church, and upon as many as heard these things.

We are living in a world today where it is not the norm anymore to tell the truth. More lies are being told than truth. The sad thing about it is that we believe the lies that are being told to us. Recently, I had the opportunity to watch an interview of a well-known gospel singer who received praise for coming out of the closet of homosexuality. Pastors and black leaders praised him for no longer living a lie. However, he never once considered repenting for his sin. He chose to continue to live in sin. Furthermore, it was embraced and applauded. Not one minister spoke out against his sin or thought repentance was in order. We should always love the individual, but never accept the sin. Regardless of what it is, sin is sin in the eyes of God. When we accept the sin, that is conforming to a sinful world.

Similarly, hearing the truth is never enough, reading the truth is not enough, and believing and speaking it is not enough. We have to hear, know, speak, believe and do what the truth says. Truth provides the clearest and most precise instructions we will ever receive. The truth is not a recipe; you cannot add a little of this and a little of that. You cannot take away this or that because it offends someone or because someone disagrees with it. The book of Revelation tells us that we cannot add or take away from the Word of God and if we do, we will face plagues and eternal damnation. That is the truth. Revelation 22:18-19, "For I testify unto every man that heareth the words of the prophecy of this book, If any man shall add unto these things, God shall add unto him the plagues that are written in this book: [19] And if any man shall take away from the words of the book of this prophecy, God shall take away his part out of the book of life, and out of the holy city, and from the things which are written in this book." As a result, our biggest struggle with the truth is that it forces change or creates denial. However, we need to be careful about whom we are hearing the Word of truth from, because not all ministers are called by God. The enemy sends out his team to preach and deceive. John 10:10, "The thief cometh not, but for to steal, and to kill, and to destroy: I am come that they might have life, and that they might have it more abundantly." Jesus tells us in John 10:8, "All that ever came before me are thieves and robbers: but the sheep did not hear them."

Besides, the reason most of us do not want to live according to the truth is that we want to do what we want to do. We want to do what the majority is doing, what the world is doing and what is most pleasing to our flesh. We struggle living a life of lies pretending to be what we are not, doing what we should not be doing and being deceived in the process.

For this reason, we find ourselves struggling on a daily basis, based on the choices we have made from lies. However, one day we will have to cross that bridge and face the truth. When we do, there will be consequences to the lies that we have lived. If you do not believe this, look at the book of Judges. It is about the children of God who did what they wanted to do according to lies, but the result was God's judgment.

God has not changed. God does not care what laws are passed or what the majority believes and wants. God still requires two things from His people when sin is committed: confession of their sin and a heart of repentance for their sins. If we were not living under grace today, we too would receive God's judgment. We do not have to struggle to live in truth according to John 16:13, "Howbeit when he, the Spirit of truth, is come, he will guide you into all truth: for he shall not speak of himself; but whatsoever he shall hear, that shall he speak: and he will shew you things to come." We can make a difference by being obedient to the voice of God or disobedient to the voice of God causing the difference we make to be positive or negative. The question is: Will we make a difference by doing the right thing or will we make a difference by doing our own thing?

Meanwhile, some of us plan to sin; then if anyone questions us, we lie and become defensive. Sometimes it takes a storm in our life to cause us to walk in the spirit of obedience. We are quick to obey man, but quick to question God. In the book of Acts, the disciples declared that they would, "Obey God rather than man;" Acts 5:29, "Then, Peter and the other Apostles answered and said, we ought to obey God rather than men."

God's Word is substance while man's word is like the wind; it will never withstand the storms and tests of life. Romans 6 provides some insight into the disciples' decisions to obey God. Romans 6:16, "Know ye not, that to whom ye yield yourselves servants to obey, his servants ye are to whom ye obey; whether of sin unto death, or of obedience unto righteousness?" Therefore, it was a choice of death or righteousness made by the disciples, and it is the same choice for us today.

It took one man's sin (Adam) for us to be separated from God and lose eternal life. Romans 5:19, "For as by one man's disobedience many were made sinners, so by the obedience of one shall many be made righteous." It took one man's obedience and righteousness (Jesus), for us to have a relationship with God and have everlasting life. Hebrews 5:8, "Though he were a Son, yet learned he obedience by the things which he suffered." Obedience is not easy; we can be obedient, but we cannot do it under our power and strength. We are not that different from Sodom or Nineveh; we are just living under the dispensation of grace.

Incidentally, to avoid conforming to a sinful world, we have to take heed to 2 Corinthians 10:5-6, "Casting down imaginations, and every high thing that exalteth itself against the knowledge of God, and bringing into captivity every thought to the obedience of Christ; [6] And having in a readiness to revenge all disobedience, when your obedience is fulfilled." As well as 2 Chronicles 7:14, "If my people, which are called by my name, shall humble themselves, and pray, and seek my face, and turn from their wicked ways; then will

I hear from heaven, and will forgive their sin, and will heal their land."

Furthermore, the sins that we commit are as natural as the rain that falls from the sky. No matter how bad we want to stop sinning and do the right thing, the power of the flesh is too strong without the Holy Spirit operating within us. Zechariah 4:6: "...Not by might nor by power, but by My Spirit, says the Lord of hosts." Without the power of God operating within us, a losing battle of sin will continue, according to the Word of God in Romans 7.

> Romans 7:14-20
> For we know that the law is spiritual: but I am carnal, sold under sin.[15] For that which I do I allow not: for what I would, that do I not; but what I hate, that do I . [16] If then I do that which I would not, I consent unto the law that it is good. [17] Now then it is no more I that do it, but sin that dwelleth in me. [18] For I know that in me (that is, in my flesh), dwelleth no good thing: for to will is present with me; but how to perform that which is good I find not.[19] For the good that I would I do not: but the evil which I would not, that I do. [20] Now if I do that I would not, it is no more I that do it, but sin that dwelleth in me.

By the way, it is not a revelation that all ten of the commandments are being broken every day without a heart of repentance. Unfortunately, it is a position of sin once held by all believers according to Ephesians 2:2, "Wherein in time past ye walked according to the course of this world, according to the prince of the power of the air, the spirit that now worketh in the children of disobedience." Table 7 is an illustration of how we break the Ten Commandments.

TABLE 7 TEN COMMANDMENTS

No.	Ten Commandments	Continues to be Broken by:
1	Deuteronomy 5:7. You shall have no other gods before me.	Putting material posses-sions, children, spouses, jobs, careers, titles, money, and positions before God.
2	Deuteronomy 5:8-10. You shall not make for yourself an idol in the form of anything in heaven above or on the earth beneath or in the waters below. [9]You shall not bow down to them or worship them; for I, the Lord your God, am a jealous God, punishing the children for the sin of the fathers to third generation of those who hate me, [10] but showing love to a thou-sand generations of those who love me and keep my commandments.	Worshipping pastors, leaders, athletes, and celebrities.
3	Deuteronomy 5:11. You shall not misuse the name of the Lord your God, for the Lord will not hold anyone guiltless who misuses his name.	A total disrespect for the name of the Lord. Used in jokes, swearing, and broken promises.
4	Deuteronomy 5:12. Observe the Sabbath day by keeping it holy, as the Lord your God has commanded you.	Engaging in activities that give personal plea-sure on the Sabbath day.
5	Deuteronomy 5:16. Honor your father and your mother, as the Lord your God has commanded you, so that you may live long and that it may go well with you in the land the Lord your God is giving you.	Honor and respect for parents is quickly becoming a thing of the past. Children today have little or no respect for their parents. Honor has been replaced with a spirit of entitlement.

No.	Ten Commandments	Continues to be Broken by:
6	Deuteronomy 5:17. You shall not murder.	Murders are increasing every year at the hands of young adults and children who have no fear of God.
7	Deuteronomy 5:18. You shall not commit adultery.	The marriage vow is no longer taken seriously by couples inside and outside of the church. Adultery is being committed with no fear of the consequences.
8	Deuteronomy 5:19. You shall not steal.	Acts of theft are everywhere we look.
9	Deuteronomy 5:20. You shall not give false testimony against your neighbor.	We are guilty of doing whatever helps us to look innocent, even at the cost of losing a neighbor as a friend.
10	Deuteronomy 5:21. You shall not covet your neighbor's wife. You shall not set your desire on your neighbor's house, or land... or anything that belongs to your neighbor.	We are witnessing the greatest lust ever for that which we do not have. The words "enough" and "contentment" have escaped our vocabularies as we continue to lust for more.

It is true we cannot keep the commandments; they keep us under the law, and the law is bondage without grace. In fact, if we break one, we break them all. Matthew 5:19, "Whosoever therefore shall break one of these least commandments, and shall teach men so, he shall be called the least in the kingdom of heaven: but whosoever shall do and teach them, the same shall be called great in the kingdom of heaven." Nevertheless, we the once strong and proud African-Americans are committing crimes at an all-time high, breaking laws, conforming to this world, and committing sin at an alarming rate according to the statistics in Table 8, Crimes and Sins and Table 9, FBI 2011 Crime Statistics.

TABLE 8 CRIMES AND SINS

Crimes, Sins, and Conforming Ways	**Statistics**
Homicide	A 2012 study by the Department of Justice's Office of Juvenile Justice and Delinquency Prevention revealed that in 2010 black youths committed six times more murders, three times more rapes, 10 times more robberies and three times more assaults than did their white counterparts.[1]
Divorce	The African-American community has the lowest marriage rate in America and the highest out of wedlock childbirth rate. But on top of these depressing numbers, the Census Bureau figures released last month show that while everyone else's divorce rate went down, black women between the ages of 50-59 were more likely to divorce. Our divorce rate went up to 48%. In addition, black women have the highest chance of their first marriage ending within ten years, at 47%.[2]

Crimes, Sins, and Conforming Ways	Statistics
Incarceration	Based on current rates of first incarceration, an estimated 32% of black males will enter State or Federal prison during their lifetime, compared to 17% of Hispanic males and 5.9% of white males. At midyear 2007, there were 4,618 black-male sentenced prisoners per 100,000 black males in the United States, compared to 1,747 Hispanic male sentenced prisoners per 100,000 Hispanic males and 773 white male sentenced prisoners per 100,000 white males.[3]

TABLE 9 FBI 2011 CRIME STATISTICS

Offense charged	Total arrests			Percent distribution		
	Total	White	Black	Total	White	Black
TOTAL	9,499,725	6,578,133	2,697,539	100.0	69.2	28.4
Murder and no negligence manslaughter	8,341	4,000	4,149	100.0	48.0	49.7
Forcible rape	14,611	9,504	4,811	100.0	65.0	32.9
Robbery	82,436	35,443	45,827	100.0	43.0	55.6
Aggravated assault	305,220	194,981	102,597	100.0	63.9	33.6
Burglary	227,899	151,934	72,244	100.0	66.7	31.7
Larceny-theft	977,743	670,768	281,197	100.0	68.6	28.8
Motor vehicle theft	50,902	32,575	17,250	100.0	64.0	33.9
Arson	8,965	6,479	2,302	100.0	72.3	25.7
Violent crime[2]	410,608	243,928	157,384	100.0	59.4	38.3
Property crime[2]	1,265,509	861,756	372,993	100.0	68.1	29.5
Other assaults	952,421	625,330	304,083	100.0	65.7	31.9
Forgery and counterfeiting	53,791	35,239	17,695	100.0	65.5	32.9
Fraud	127,664	84,919	40,621	100.0	66.5	31.8
Embezzlement	12,454	8,155	4,032	100.0	65.5	32.4
Stolen property; buying, receiving, possessing	71,727	47,434	23,191	100.0	66.1	32.3
Vandalism	182,482	132,850	45,055	100.0	72.8	24.7

[102]http://www.fbi.gov/about-us/cjis/ucr/crime-in-the-u.s/2011/crime-in-the-u.s.-2011/tables/table-43

Offense charged	Total arrests			Percent distribution		
	Total	White	Black	Total	White	Black
Weapons; carrying, possessing, etc.	117,820	68,453	47,515	100.0	58.1	40.3
Prostitution and commercialized vise	44,090	23,555	19,227	100.0	53.4	43.6
Sex offenses (except forcible rape and prostitution)	52,891	38,422	13,189	100.0	72.6	24.9
Drug abuse violations	1,171,866	783,564	371,248	100.0	66.9	31.7
Gambling	6,507	1,937	4,351	100.0	29.8	66.9
Offenses against the family and children	87,586	56,973	28,183	100.0	65.0	32.2
Driving under the influence	924,210	788,175	111,480	100.0	85.3	12.1
Liquor laws	380,663	312,106	51,446	100.0	82.0	13.5
Drunkenness	413,723	339,019	64,268	100.0	81.9	15.5
Disorderly conduct	447,201	281,531	153,840	100.0	63.0	34.4
Vagrancy	22,375	12,989	8,794	100.0	58.1	39.3
All other offenses (except traffic)	2,693,823	1,794,893	837,095	100.0	66.6	31.1
Suspicion	1,150	634	506	100.0	55.1	44.0
Curfew and loitering law violations	59,164	36,271	21,343	100.0	61.3	36.1

Generally speaking, the crime statistics of blacks can be reduced significantly by going back to the original African-American baseline of fear and reverence for God. It is time for us to bend our knees unto a holy and righteous God, Ephesians 3.

Ephesians 3:14-21
For this cause I bow my knees unto the Father of our Lord Jesus Christ, |15| Of whom the whole family in heaven and earth is named , |16| That he would grant you, according to the riches of his glory, to be strengthened with might by his Spirit in the inner man;|17| That Christ may dwell in your hearts by faith; that ye, being rooted and grounded in love, |18| May be able to comprehend with all saints what is the breadth, and length, and depth, and height;|19| And to know the love of Christ, which passeth knowledge, that ye might be filled with all the fulness of God. |20| Now unto him that is able to do exceeding abundantly above all that we ask or think, according to the power that worketh in us, |21| Unto him be glory in the church by Christ Jesus throughout all ages, world without end. Amen.

In other words, we have sat back and allowed the world to redefine sin for us to the point that sin is not sin and wrong is right. Why? Because we are spiritually weak. We have Christians in the church who are confused about who they are and whose they are. Christians who do not believe they are children of the King. They are the victims of an identity crisis. However, what we believe as Christians and what we stand for was built on the Rock, the uncompromising Word of God. Nevertheless, that which the world believes was built on sand and it shifts and changes every day. Sand cannot withstand the numerous businesses closing every day, the flood of jobs being lost every hour, and the wind of economic changes and disasters that are slowly eroding personal finances, wiping out all that people have saved. However, when we stand on the Rock, Jesus will shower us with His blessings, flood us with His grace, and when He blows, we will experience His presence, glory, and all-consuming power.

In essence, those in the world define themselves by what they have, but we define ourselves by Who we have. We have Jesus Christ, the Rock. If we look at the Word, it has not changed; if we look at Christ, He has not changed, and neither have His expectations of a Christian. It is disturbing to be in a position to have everything you need and not know it. Everything we need has already been provided for us. All we have to do is ask, trust, believe and receive.

As African-Americans, we are not influencing the world in a Christian way. On the contrary, the world is influencing us. We are conforming to the ways of the world to the point that it is hard to distinguish between a Christian family and a non-Christian family. We want to be known as children of God, be in the will of God and be a proud race again. We should desire for the Lord to know us by name and to be one of those who will receive eternal life with the Lord, as discussed in the book of Matthew.

Matthew 7:21-27
Not everyone that saith unto me, Lord, Lord, shall enter into the kingdom of heaven; but he that doeth the will of my Father which is in heaven. [22] Many will say to me in that day, Lord, Lord, have we not prophesied in thy name? and in thy name have cast out devils? and in thy name done many wonderful works? [23] And then will I profess unto them, I never knew you: depart from me, ye that work iniquity. [24] Therefore whosoever heareth these sayings of mine, and doeth them, I will liken him unto a wise man,

which built his house upon a rock: [25] And the rain descended, and the floods came, and the winds blew, and beat upon that house; and it fell not: for it was founded upon a rock. [26] And every one that heareth these sayings of mine, and doeth them not, shall be likened unto a foolish man, which built his house upon the sand: [27] And the rain descended, and the floods came, and the winds blew, and beat upon that house; and it fell: and great was the fall of it.

In the church, we have learned some of the attributes of Christ and used them to deceive people about who we are; but those in the world are not easily fooled by our pretentious ways. If we swim in water, it does not make us fishes. If we bury our feet in sand, it does not make us plants. If we fly in a plane, it does not mean we can fly like a bird. Therefore, coming to church does not mean we are Christians. We are just non-repentant sinners who attend church until we accept Jesus as our Lord. *and in the area's that we struggle ask God for His help.*

We should do all we can to be obedient to the Word of God. It would be better for us not to know what to do than to know what to do and not do it. To whom much is given, much is required. The world would not be confused about our identity if our attitude and love towards people were the same at home, work, and in the streets as it is in the church on Sunday mornings.

If we are going to call ourselves Christians, let us begin and continue to do what Christians are called to do; act like our Father and display the attributes of Christ. Love like Him, forgive like Him and allow Him to be Lord in our lives by turning everything over to Him and trusting and believing in Him, His Word, and His promises.

Besides, as Christians we do not have to worry about identity theft. Our identity, our worth, our power, our grace and mercy is all wrapped up in Christ. The blood of Jesus has sealed us, and we have a covenant with Him that can never be broken.

The enemy cannot steal our identity, but we can allow him to take it by believing his lies and craftiness. Yes, the enemy is dumb. He has no new tricks, no new weapons, but we are dumber if we do not accept the gift of eternal life and God's divine protection and provision.

God has given us a new name and a new identity with Kingdom benefits. In

John 13:34-35, "A new commandment I give unto you, That ye love one another; as I have loved you, that ye also love one another. [35] By this shall all men know that ye are my disciples, if ye have love one to another."

Similarly, the God that we worship and serve is not pleased with the direction this world is going. Our sins and lack of fear of the true and living God are reflected in our sinful lifestyle and confirmed in Romans 1.

Romans 1:26-32

For this cause God gave them up unto vile affections: for even their women did change the natural use into that which is against nature: [27] And likewise also the men, leaving the natural use of the woman, burned in their lust one toward another; men with men working that which is unseemly, and receiving in themselves that recompense of their error which was meet. [28] And even as they did not like to retain God in their knowledge, God gave them over to a reprobate mind, to do those things which are not convenient; [29] Being filled with all unrighteousness, fornication, wickedness, covetousness, maliciousness; full of envy, murder, debate, deceit, malignity; whisperers, [30] Backbiters, haters of God, despiteful, proud, boasters, inventors of evil things, disobedient to parents, [31] Without understanding, covenant breakers, without natural affection, implacable, unmerciful: [32] Who knowing the judgment of God, that they which commit such things are worthy of death, not only do the same, but have pleasure in them that do them.

Before we go out to preach the gospel and share the love of Christ to the lost, we must understand that we are living in a world that is seeking a god that they want and not the God Who is. The World has a totally different viewpoint, opinion, and vision of who God is and what God will and will not do. It is not that the world does not want or have a god. They do not want the God we know. They want a god they are seeking, in accordance with the attributes of God described in Table 10.

TABLE 10 ATTRIBUTES OF GOD

No.	The God Christians Serve is:	The God that the World is Seeking:
1.	An all-knowing God.	Is powerless and non-existent.
2.	Alpha and Omega. The Beginning and the End. The First and the Last.	Was created and made for them in their vile imaginations.
3.	Holy and Righteous.	Is Predictable and limited.
4.	The First and the Last	Overlooks sins.
5.	The Great I Am.	Makes them happy and feel good.
6.	Creator and Maker of all things.	Changes with each generation.
7.	By right the supreme and absolute Ruler of all things, both in the visible and invisible world.	Understands that the world is different today, and the Bible is outdated.
8.	Who He is by divine right	Gives them what they want.
9.	A God that does not extend into space, He is a God that contains space.	Is willing to change with them.
10.	Outside of all things, inside of all things, and around all things.	Sends everyone to Heaven, regardless of his or her sinful and lustful lifestyle.
11.	Imminent, which means we do not have to go anywhere to find God. It is impossible to think of the place where God is not.	Is one they can serve when and how they want to and question His whereabouts when things go wrong in their lives.
12.	A God that controls the ocean, sun, moon, stars, animals, and all other things.	Allows man to be in charge. Is available only when there is a need.

9. VISION AND PURPOSE

Vision and purpose are two very powerful words that must be incorporated into the vocabulary and daily life of African-Americans. These two words must be taught, understood and practiced every day to their fullness in the lives of all African-Americans for healing and restoration. They are critical to the black race for moving forward in life.

Without a vision and without having a defined purpose in life, there will be no consistent progress made in African-American communities. Today, so many young people with no goals in life are living without purpose. Unfortunately, this has carried over into the lives of adults who are content with just having a job and receiving a paycheck every week. If the parents and adults are not dreaming, planning, and writing their visions, how can we expect the younger generation to succeed in society? In fact, we cannot expect anyone to succeed in life who does not take the time to write their visions and set goals for their lives and their families.

The Word of God tells us in Habakkuk 2:2, "And the LORD answered me, and said, Write the vision, and make it plain upon tables, that he may run that readeth it. If God has told us to write the vision, then we need to write the vision. Until a vision is written, it is just another wasted idea of words expressed without meaning, purpose, and accountability.

Besides, we are all born with a purpose and a journey
that must be completed. Once we understand them, we are to
pass them on to our children and the children around us. Too
often, though, history has to start and stop, repeating itself
until the lesson is learned. When we ignore the lessons of history, we are ignoring the things we need for ourselves today.
[103] The major concern within the black community today is
that there are only a few of us teaching the lessons of our past
journeys to this generation. Consequently, too many African-
Americans are walking around living without purpose and
vision, with no clear path of success in their sight.

Subsequently, if African-Americans want to avoid per-
ishing, they have to become visionaries, not just for themselves, but also for their families, communities, and race.
Scripture tells us in Proverbs 29:18, "Where there is no vision,
the people perish: but he that keepeth the law, happy is he."
Therefore, blacks should not be stunned by their failures and
unhappiness within our race or the lack of progress that has
not been made in this society compared to the progress that
other races have made.

Regardless of what we, as African-Americans, have gone
through (past or present), we are aware of the promise and
hope of Romans 8:28, "And we know that all things work
together for good to them that love God, to them who are the
called according to his purpose." This scripture is not for us
to escape our responsibilities or avoid any consequences, but
to bring us peace and increase our faith by knowing as long
as we are in our Father's will and continue to call on Jesus,
He will work it out for us.

As a rule we need to know who is speaking into our spirit,
because we are guilty of destroying our homes, careers, and
families from listening and acting upon words of prophecy

[103]Bertice Berry. *The Ties That Bind*. (New York: The Doubleday
Publishing Group; 2009), 170.

that were not from men and women of God. In spite of Jeremiah's warnings in Jeremiah 14:14, "Then the LORD said unto me, The prophets prophesy lies in my name: I sent them not, neither have I commanded them, neither spake unto them: they prophesy unto you a false vision and divination, and a thing of naught, and the deceit of their heart." We have heard and received lies, lies that have changed the direction of lives. Lies that have created hate and un-forgiveness in the hearts of African-Americans. Lies that have created a wall between races, communities, and families, just for profit or title recognition.

Nevertheless, we have a vision and purpose trapped inside of us. In other words, we are pregnant with purpose and vision. We need to open our eyes to the fact that the enemy (Satan) will use anyone or anything to abort the vision God has for us. As a result, we may never see our purpose fulfilled per Jeremiah 23:16, "Thus saith the Lord of hosts, Hearken not unto the words of the prophets that prophesy unto you: they make you vain: they speak a vision of their own heart, and not out of the mouth of the Lord."

Regardless of our race's past, future, or present, God has given all of us gifts that need to be nurtured, matured, and stirred up within us for the Kingdom of God. Just as Paul instructed Timothy, we too need to be educated as to what is within each of us for the glory of God.

2 Timothy 1:4-14
Greatly desiring to see thee, being mindful of thy tears, that I may be filled with joy; [5] When I call to remembrance the unfeigned faith that is in thee, which dwelt first in thy grandmother Lois, and thy mother Eunice; and I am persuaded that in thee also. [6] Wherefore I put thee in remembrance that thou stir up the gift of God, which is in thee by the putting on of my hands.[7] For God hath not given us the spirit

of fear; but of power, and of love, and of a sound mind. [8] Be not thou therefore ashamed of the testimony of our Lord, nor of me his prisoner: but be thou partaker of the afflictions of the gospel according to the power of God; [9] Who hath saved us, and called us with an holy calling, not according to our works, but according to his own purpose and grace, which was given us in Christ Jesus before the world began , [10] But is now made manifest by the appearing of our Saviour Jesus Christ, who hath abolished death, and hath brought life and immortality to light through the gospel:[11] Whereunto I am appointed a preacher, and an apostle, and a teacher of the Gentiles.[12] For the which cause I also suffer these things: nevertheless I am not ashamed : for I know whom I have believed , and am persuaded that he is able to keep that which I have committed unto him against that day.[13] Hold fast the form of sound words, which thou hast heard of me, in faith and love which is in Christ Jesus.[14] That good thing which was committed unto thee keep by the Holy Ghost which dwelleth in us.

God calls each of us to be visionary leaders, but we must allow the vision to be born out of our spirit. Other ideas can lead us away from dependence on God to a self-based psychology designed to give us more power, prosperity, and significance based on the principles and beliefs of man. We must always beware of anything that puts the burden of performance on us rather than God. The promise God has for us is pregnant in us with divine possibility, yet integrated with human responsibility, with a will to do or not do the will of God.

It is no secret that our culture emphasizes materialism. Violent disrespect for life is everywhere. We are bombarded with messages telling us how successful, beautiful, loved, respected, smart, and happy we will be, if we buy *this* or *that*.

"Acquiring" and "having" are touted as the purposes of life. Nevertheless, people with all levels of financial resources are depressed, discouraged, angry, and empty. Things can go very wrong quickly when our children are brought up to live just for themselves with the belief that their main goal is to have wealth, power, and prestige. The ubiquitous materialism of our culture makes it difficult to prioritize our children's inner lives and maintain their connection to the universe. That is exactly what we must do. The blueprints for discovering our purpose can be found inside, in the soul where God lives, and outside, in God's magnificent natural world. When children trust that all life has a purpose, they respect and appreciate themselves and the people around them. Kindness, empathy, compassion, and love grow from appreciation and respect, and in turn create more of both. When parents and children incorporate this principle into their lives, a spiritual circle has begun.[104]

A spiritual circle must be a continuous process. It cannot be something we start being on fire about doing and stop before we fulfill our purpose or complete our journey. The enemy has the patience of Job to wait for us to become discouraged and defeated.

Furthermore, the purpose of children is found in God reproducing His image in humankind all over the earth so they can advance His kingdom. Children have a spiritual reason for existence, not just a biological, physiological, or familiar reason. God wants parents to transfer a theocentric, God-centered worldview to children. Raising Kingdom kids means giving your children a Kingdom perspective so they will align their decisions with His will throughout their lives. This, in turn, will bring glory to God as they reflect His rule on earth. To raise your children with a Kingdom perspective is to love them fully. They truly need to learn how to be responsible,

---

[104]Mimi Doe and Marsha Walch. *10 Principles for Spiritual Parenting.* (New York, NY: Harper Collins Publishers, Inc.; 1998.), 38.

patient, hardworking, and spiritually minded. Those are the greatest love gifts you can give to your children, because those gifts of love will enable them to be successful in life.[105]

To illustrate, I have learned to speak and confess the Word of God to myself. It helps me to stay strong in the Lord, and it confirms in my spirit who I am in Christ, regardless of what others may do or say to discourage or defeat me. This same concept can be used to teach other blacks who are challenged with knowing whom they are to write a personal confession statement from the Word of God like the example below.

> Personal Confession Statement:
> I am a new creation; I am healed of all sickness and diseases because He sent His Word and healed me, and delivered me from their destructions. The Lord is my shepherd; I shall not want. The Lord is my light and my salvation; whom shall I fear? The Lord is the strength of my life; of whom shall I be afraid? My God shall supply all my needs according to His riches in glory by Christ Jesus. I am of God; I am his child, and I have overcome them, because He who is in me is greater than he who is in the world. He has delivered me from the power of darkness and conveyed me into the kingdom of the Son of His love, and these signs will follow me because I believe: In His name I will cast out demons; I will speak with new tongues.
>
> I have been crucified with Christ; it is no longer I who live, but Christ lives in me; and the life which I now live in the flesh I live by faith in the Son of God, who loved me and gave Himself for me. Because I have confessed my sins, He is faithful and just to

---

[105]Tony Evans and Chrystal Evans Hurst. *Kingdom Woman*. (Carol Stream, Illinois: Tyndale House Publishers, Inc.; 2013), 164.

forgive me my sins and to cleanse me from all unrighteousness. Blessed be the God and Father of our Lord
Jesus Christ, who has blessed me with every spiritual
blessing in the heavenly places in Christ.

I have overcome him by the blood of the Lamb and
by the word of my testimony. I am a doer of the Word,
and not a hearer only, deceiving myself. He, the Spirit
of truth, has come, and He will guide me into all
truth; for He will not speak on His own authority, but
whatever He hears He will speak; and He will tell me
things to come. There is therefore now no condemnation to me for I am in Christ Jesus, and I do not walk
according to the flesh, but according to the Spirit.

I have been raised up with Him, and He has made me
to sit together in the heavenly places in Christ Jesus,
but what does it say? "The Word is near me, in my
mouth and in my heart" (that is, the word of faith
which we preach). The God that I serve is able to do
exceedingly abundantly, above all that I ask or think,
according to the power that works in me. I will not
live by bread alone, but by every word that proceeds
from the mouth of God for with God nothing will be
impossible. What then shall I say to these things? If
God is for me, who can be against me?

At the same time, executing purpose requires planning.
There is one concern that I see when planning is done by well-
meaning believers who do not include God. If God is not the
originator and director of the plan, then that plan is doomed
for failure. When Jesus said, "He came only to do the will of
the Father," He would not consider doing anything that was
not what the Father wanted, no matter how good or righteous
it might have appeared to be. Proverbs 16:9, "A man's heart

deviseth his way: but the Lord directeth his steps." God must give us the vision for what He calls us to do. After we have the vision, we must ask Him if He wants us to take action on that vision and what the action steps entail. The Lord wants to direct each step of our planning process, because He already knows where we are going. It is our responsibility to seek Him to find out His mind on the matter. It is only when we remain connected to the source (Jesus) that we can be assured of putting God's plan into place. We do not want to have an experience like Saul on the road to Damascus in Acts 26.

Acts 26:12-23
Whereupon as I went to Damascus with authority and commission from the chief priests, [13] At midday, O king, I saw in the way a light from heaven, above the brightness of the sun, shining round about me and them which journeyed with me. [14] And when we were all fallen to the earth, I heard a voice speaking unto me, and saying in the Hebrew tongue, Saul, Saul, why persecutest thou me? it is hard for thee to kick against the pricks. [15] And I said, Who art thou, Lord? And he said , I am Jesus whom thou persecutest .[16] But rise , and stand upon thy feet: for I have appeared unto thee for this purpose, to make thee a minister and a witness both of these things which thou hast seen , and of those things in the which I will appear unto thee;[17] Delivering thee from the people, and from the Gentiles, unto whom now I send thee,[18] To open their eyes, and to turn them from darkness to light, and from the power of Satan unto God, that they may receive forgiveness of sins, and inheritance among them which are sanctified by faith that is in me.[19] Whereupon, O king Agrippa, I was not disobedient unto the heavenly vision:[20] But shewed first unto them of Damascus, and at Jerusalem, and

throughout all the coasts of Judaea, and then to the Gentiles, that they should repent and turn to God, and do works meet for repentance.[21] For these causes the Jews caught me in the temple, and went about to kill me. [22] Having therefore obtained help of God, I continue unto this day, witnessing both to small and great, saying none other things than those which the prophets and Moses did say should come: [23] That Christ should suffer, and that he should be the first that should rise from the dead, and should shew light unto the people, and to the Gentiles.

At the same time, we have allowed our wants to interfere with our purpose. Our wants have nothing to do with the vision and purpose God has for us. In fact, our wants have become obstacles to our receiving the blessings of God. We must learn to walk in the Spirit as told to us in Galatians 5:16-17, "This I say then, Walk in the Spirit, and ye shall not fulfil the lust of the flesh. [17] For the flesh lusteth against the Spirit, and the Spirit against the flesh: and these are contrary the one to the other: so that ye cannot do the things that ye would."

In other words, our wants are a reflection of what is in our hearts and what is in our heart is what we have allowed this flesh to expose. The things we are exposed to the most are the things we have a tendency to want. The things we want and desire more than God will drive us to make choices and do things that will result in consequences that are not pleasing. How can we possibly know what we want, when God's Word tells us that we do not even know what to pray for? Romans 8:26-27, "Likewise the Spirit also helpeth our infirmities: for we know not what we should pray for as we ought: but the Spirit itself maketh intercession for us with groanings which cannot be uttered. And he that searcheth the hearts knoweth what is the mind of the Spirit, because he maketh intercession for the saints according to the will of God."

That is to say that there are jobs, relationships and marriages we prayed for because we wanted them, but God said, "No" or told us to wait. Nevertheless, we did what we wanted to do. Consequently, we are now praying to get out of it. We want to leave those same jobs, relationships and marriages. How many times have we wanted a promotion or a raise more than anything? We worked hard for it until we got it. However, in the process, no one knew we were a Christian because we put God and the things of God on the backburner. We did it with no conviction or shame. These things, in many cases, have caused us to miss our purpose.

● When we realize that most of the things we seek separate us from the Lord and take us further from His will, perhaps we will begin to make some sacrifices and move some stuff and people out of our lives, allowing us to spend more time with the Lord so that we can fulfill God's will and purpose. It is only then that we can realize the vision that is waiting to be birthed in us is bigger than we are. ●

10. SEED AND HARVEST

The first thing that emanates into Christians' minds when they hear the words "seeds and harvest" are financial blessings. Financial blessings are great, but what about our time and Return On Time (ROT)? What is the return on all of the time we invest in the things we do and do not do? Time is seed that we can plant, but is also one of the most wasted and mismanaged gifts. As an African-American, I have personally witnessed numerous situations and environments where the majority of an individual's time was spent working. However, the balance of their time was wasted on unproductive and wasteful activities that profit nothing.

In the meantime, every time that God blesses us with another day, we get another 24 hours, 1,440 minutes, or 86,400 seconds to plant seeds into the lives of others. Seeds of forgiveness, grace, kindness, service, and most importantly, love. I have seen too many African-Americans giving testimonies about God being first in their lives, only to discover at the end of the day that no quality time has been allocated to spend with Him.

Furthermore, if we are going to sow love, we have to know that God is love. We cannot sow what we do not have to sow. The scripture tells us in 1 John 4:7-8, "But if we walk in the light, as he is in the light, we have fellowship one with another, and the blood of Jesus Christ his Son cleanseth us from all sin. [8] If we say that we have no sin, we deceive ourselves, and the truth is not in us." The world consists of many different organized religions, but many of them agree on one thing and that is the importance of sowing love in the life of all humans, as reflected in Table 11, Various Organized Religious Views on Love. This table represents eleven different organized religious beliefs all with a common denominator: love. However, I can assure you that they do not all define love in accordance with the scriptures in 1 John 4:7-8. Nevertheless, from a positive perspective, the importance of love is embedded and taught in their religion.

TABLE 11 VARIOUS ORGANIZED RELIGIUS VIEWS ON LOVE[106]

No.	Organized Religion	Love Paraphrases
1.	Christian	God is love; you are God's and children of the highest.
2.	Shinto	Love is the receptacle of the Lord.
3.	Zoroastrian	Man is the beloved of the Lord, and you should love him in return.
4.	Judaic	Thou shall love the Lord thy God with all thy heart and thy neighbor as thyself.
5.	Sikh	God will regenerate those in whose hands there is love.
6.	Buddha	Let a man cultivate toward the whole world a heart of love.
7.	Tao	Heaven arms with love those it would not see destroyed.
8.	Islam	Love is this, that thou shouldst account thyself very little and God very great.

---

[106]Wayne W. Dyer. *There's a Spiritual Solution to Every Problem.* (New York, NY: Harper Collins Publishers; 2001), 163.

No.	Organized Religion	Love Paraphrases
9.	Baha'i	If you love me not, my love can no wise reach thee.
10	Confucian	To love all men is the greatest benevolence.
11.	Hindu	One can best worship the Lord through love.

At the same time, as seed planters we must keep in mind that life does not always appear to be fair because it is not fair. However, the mistake we have made is trying to earn our treasure here on earth. That was never the plan of God. God has always expected to be number one in our lives. He wants us to get rid of whatever keeps us from putting Him at the top. Mark 10:21, "Then Jesus beholding him loved him, and said unto him, One thing thou lackest: go thy way, sell whatsoever thou hast, and give to the poor, and thou shalt have treasure in heaven: and come, take up the cross, and follow me."

Similarly, when we are faithful in sowing our time and love into the lives of others, God is faithful to His words in Galatians that whatsoever we sow, we will one day reap all the blessings in God's Harvest, Figure 8.

Galatians 6:7-10
Be not deceived; God is not mocked: for whatsoever a man soweth, that shall he also reap. [8] For he that soweth to his flesh shall of the flesh reap corruption; but he that soweth to the Spirit shall of the Spirit reap life everlasting. [9] And let us not be weary in well doing: for in due season we shall reap, if we faint not. [10] As we have therefore opportunity, let us do good unto all men, especially unto them who are of the household of faith.

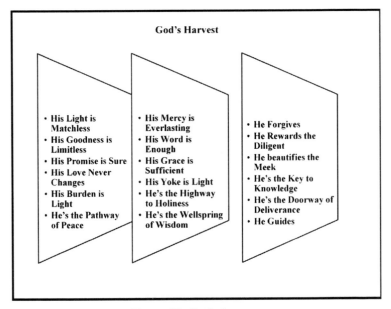

Figure 18. God's harvest.

11. WHAT ARE THE ANSWERS?

W hat Are The Answers To Healing And Restoring An African-American race that has hundreds of years of pain and economical disadvantages? From a biblical point of view, it begins with having a relationship with Christ. I am afraid it does not get any more straightforward than having Christ in charge of our lives. Jesus prayed to the Father in John 17 that the love God has for Him could be experienced by us.

John 17:24-26
Father, I will that they also, whom thou hast given me, be with me where I am; that they may behold my glory, which thou hast given me: for thou lovedst me before the foundation of the world. [25] O righteous Father, the world hath not known thee: but I have known thee, and these have known that thou hast sent me. [26] And I have declared unto them thy name, and will declare it: that the love wherewith thou hast loved me may be in them, and I in them.

By the same token, if we as African-Americans are going to make it and overcome the obstacles and weapons that are waiting for us, we have to stop putting so much emphasis on religion and put more emphasis on Jesus and our faith. We must make up our minds that no matter what it is going to cost us, we will have a relationship with God and we will faith the good fight of faith.

Unfortunately, many blacks have never experienced a good, honest relationship. Therefore, they have no baseline to compare a relationship. That is because our first relationship was with our mothers and fathers. Moreover, if our mother or father was not trustworthy, caring, loving, and supportive, we grew up with trust and abandonment issues that have carried over into our adult lives.

Additionally, we have had relationship issues in our personal lives that have hindered us from trusting God and having a meaningful and thriving relationship with the one true and living God that gave His only begotten Son for you and me to live and have everlasting life.

For instance, we have become angry and blamed God for deaths, sicknesses, diseases and everything we thought He should have done and did not do. It is amazing that we cannot understand the concept of a relationship with a God that we cannot see. However, we can channel our anger and disappointment, relationally, toward a God we cannot see when things fall apart in our lives. As a rule, if it nonsense to have a relationship with a God we cannot see, then it should be nonsense to be angry with a God we cannot see.

Regardless of our disappointments with man, we cannot compare what a human has done to us versus what God has promised. We serve a God that cannot lie, a God that we can call on any time, a God that will never leave us or forsake us and who will be with us until the end of the world. There is a point in time for us to learn the voice of God, know the voice of God, obey the voice of God, trust and believe what we read and hear in His Word. When this is accomplished, we can have a committed relationship with a loving, caring, powerful, and jealous God, a God who does not want to be second to anything or anyone.

To explain, one of the definitions for the word "relation-ship" is "a connection between persons by blood or marriage." As Christians, we can enter into a relationship with God by both blood and marriage. By blood, thanks to the blood that was shed by Jesus on Calvary for you and me; and by mar-riage because as Christians, we are the church and the bride of Christ. Yes, the Church is a living, breathing organism that has a relationship with God that is created on a foundation of seven things, Table 12:

TABLE 12 FOUNDATION TO A RELATIONSHIP

No.	Foundation	Description
1	Communication	Hearing and responding to Jesus' voice is the key to having a two-way relationship with God. It is the differ-ence between having religion and a relationship.
2	Commitment	Commitment is a choice. We make time for those we are committed to every day!
3	Compassion	No longer seeing Him as one to be feared, as much as one to know intimately.
4	Caring	Mutual respect and care. Seek His face to see Him for His love and tenderness toward us as His children.
5	Giving and Serving	Seeking the face of God not for what He gives, but for what He already has given. Serving with love and joy.
6	Love	God. Agape. Unconditional.
7	Provision	When we enter into a relationship with the Lord, we shall receive grace and mercy in all aspects of our lives.

Before we set any expectations to receive the blessings of the Lord, we must have a relationship with God, and we cannot have that relationship without Jesus. I am talking about a committed relationship, where we walk throughout the day with Jesus on our minds, go the bed with Jesus on our minds, wake up with Jesus on our minds; invite Him into our conversations and every decision we make. Our relationship with Jesus serves as a mirror for our children and shows them an example of how spirituality and daily life are merged. Everything we do or say, every habit we have, our tone of voice, our expressions, all teach our children what the world is and how they fit. What they see in us is a mirror of the bigger world. What they see in us is a reflection of who they are and who they are to become. What you do now for and with your child is very important; what you do with your life also sends profound messages that will remain with them throughout their lives. This responsibility need not be a burden; instead, it can be a joyous adventure for both parents and children. As you put your spirituality into everything you do, you turn each experience into an opportunity for increased good; you create your reality and your child witnesses that miracle.[107]

Generally speaking, our black kids will continue to be statistics in somebody's books and records until we learn that chastening is love, not material things. We will continue the risk of losing our kids to a sinful world until we step up our game. We need to be better parents, leaders, and concerned individuals. The Word of God does not change and the scriptures in Hebrews 12 continue to apply to us today.

Hebrews 12:5-11
And ye have forgotten the exhortation which speaketh unto you as unto children, My son, despise not

---

[107]Doe, Mimi and Marsha Walch. *10 Principles for Spiritual Parenting.* (New York, NY: Harper Collins Publishers, Inc.; 1998), 255.

thou the chastening of the Lord, nor faint when thou art rebuked of him: |6| For whom the Lord loveth he chasteneth, and scourgeth every son whom he receiveth. |7| If ye endure chastening, God dealeth with you as with sons; for what son is he whom the father chasteneth not? |8| But if ye be without chastisement, whereof all are partakers, then are ye bastards, and not sons. |9| Furthermore we have had fathers of our flesh which corrected us, and we gave them reverence: shall we not much rather be in subjection unto the Father of spirits, and live? |10| For they verily for a few days chastened us after their own pleasure; but he for our profit, that we might be partakers of his holiness. |11| Now no chastening for the present seemeth to be joyous, but grievous: nevertheless afterward it yieldeth the peaceable fruit of righteousness unto them which are exercised thereby.

Incidentally, it is true that we have a heavenly Father who knows more than what we know, regardless of our education, degrees, experience, titles, and success. We will never know more than our heavenly Father knows because He is all-knowing and ever-present. With that being said, would it not make sense to say, "Our Father knows what is best for us"? He knows what we should put on and take off. He knows what we should say or not say. He knows what we should think and should not think. He knows the places we should go and should not go. He knows what friends we should have and what friends we should avoid. He knows whom we should date and whom we should marry.

The Latin word for father is *pater*; to nourish, protect and uphold. However, our Heavenly Father gives us choices. When we make the wrong choice, it can result in unbearable consequences and serious chastisement. So the question is: How can we avoid the chastisement of our Father? We cannot! We are not that good and never will be as long as we live in these fleshly bodies. Sin without chastisement is called alienation from God. Our entire life here in this world is spent in a state of childhood and imperfection in the sight of God. Our Father tells us what to cast off and what to put on in Romans 13.

> Romans 13:12-14
>
> The night is far spent, the day is at hand: let us there-fore cast off the works of darkness, and let us put on the armour of light. |13| Let us walk honestly, as in the day; not in rioting and drunkenness, not in cham-bering and wantonness, not in strife and envying. |14| But put ye on the Lord Jesus Christ, and make not provision for the flesh, to fulfill the lusts thereof.

We should not forget that God knows every battle we have gone through and will go through in the future and He always provides a way out. It is up to us as African-Americans to take a closer look at the chastisement we are going through and remember that disappointments are God's appointments. If we read Isaiah, maybe we will stop trying to figure out God. Isaiah 55:9, "For as the heavens are higher than the earth, so are my ways higher than your ways and my thoughts than your thoughts." Tragedies can be blessings in disguise. Therefore, the correct thing to do would be to ask the Lord what He is requiring of us. In addition, we can focus on some of the meaningful words that are associated with chastise-ment in Table 13, so that we will not become discouraged when we are chastised.

TABLE 13 WORDS THAT ARE ASSOCIATED WITH
CHASTISEMENT

No.	Words	Scriptures
1.	Happy	Job 5:17–Behold, happy is the man whom God correcteth: therefore despise not thou the chastening of the Almighty:
2.	Blessed	Psalm 94:12–Blessed is the man whom thou chastenest, O LORD, and teachest him out of thy law.
3.	Loved	Proverbs 3:11-12–My son, despise not the chastening of the Lord; neither be weary of his correction: [12] For whom the Lord loveth he correcteth; even as a father the son in whom he delighteth.
4.	Repentance	Revelation 3:19–As many as I love, I rebuke and chasten: be zealous therefore, and repent.
5.	Afflicted	Psalm 119:75–I know, O Lord, that thy judgments are right, and that thou in faithfulness hast afflicted me.

To put it another way: everyone has his cross to carry that is his unique problem. However, keep in mind three words written by Saint Paul in his letters to the Corinthians, "Love never fails." Ponder these three words while asking yourself if you can think of any exceptions. "Never" means what it says; never. Whenever we are caught in a perceived problem, sending love never fails. Whatever we perceive to be our problems, we can find a solution in these three straightforward, no nonsense, no-room-for-equivocation words: love never fails. This holds true even in situations where hatred seems to be a problem. The presence of a belief in hatred is a major source of most troubles. This may seem incomprehensible, but sowing love means dissolving the illusion of hatred by becoming a delivery system for love. When we can do this, we are on the path of accessing spiritual solutions for all problems[108]

When you make the shift to sowing love in the circumstances of your life where you are encountering hate, something unique happens; first to yourself, and then to the energy field of hate. When you start to trust love and recognize that ultimately we will be one with that love, you make a huge impact on the low energy pattern of hate. Every single time that you observe anyone in the world demonstrating hate, know with complete certainty that this person feels hated. At the same time, know that this person is loved by God, since God is love. As a witness or a recipient of that hatred, you are a spark of love. If you can sow love in response to hate, you will ultimately see hate become love. Then you know with certainty that hate is only an error created by the mind of man.[109]

Nevertheless, our African American families and households would benefit greatly if we began to sow more love and less hate, and if we made some biblical affirmations that we would we be willing to stand on continuously. Likewise, create affirmations for our children and have them follow our example, as shown in Table 14, Affirmations for Adults and Children.

[108]Wayne W. Dyer. *There's a Spiritual Solution to Every Problem.* (New York, NY: Harper Collins Publishers; 2001), 159.

[109]Wayne W. Dyer. *There's a Spiritual Solution to Every Problem.* (New York, NY: Harper Collins Publishers; 2001), 162.

TABLE 14 AFFIRMATIONS[110]

No.	Adult Affirmations	Children Affirmations
1.	I am a loving mirror for my child.	Love surrounds me like a warm, snuggly coat.
2.	I find my own peace today.	I love and respect myself.
3.	My life is balanced and full of abundant blessings.	I can try again and again.
4.	I am strong, successful, and courageous.	I am a positive model for other kids.
5.	I am a creative channel for God's good; my children are living reflections of that divine energy.	When I look in the mirror, I like what I see.

~~Black~~ people today say economic power is what we need to uplift the race in America. We already have one of the biggest economies in the entire world, but we have little or no economic power, simply because we as black people use our money as the world's best consumers, but the worst investors. Economic unity is the wheel that runs a capitalistic society. People are putting economic resources together, lending and borrowing. That is the first rule of economic prosperity. Economic unity will help us when black men begin to put their economic resources together to start small businesses, start banks or manufacturing businesses. We need to use our economic resources to make political and social changes for the good of our communities.[111]

[110]Mimi Doe and Marsha Walch. *10 Principles for Spiritual Parenting.* (New York, NY: Harper Collins Publishers, Inc.; 1998), 290.

[111]Asher Ledwidge. *Saving the Black Culture A Revolution of Hope-Black Unity-Brotherly Love.* (Clermont, Florida: Self-published Asher Ledwidge; 2004), 232.

Additionally, we need to become unified, spiritually. When we speak of spiritual unity, most people say it is about unity with God. This is very true; however, the biggest problem with the human race is our disconnection from the spiritual grace of God. Our spiritual separation, our fall from the grace of God, makes us live as spiritual outlaws. Mankind's spiritual unity must consist of two equal parts: friendship with his Creator and friendship with his fellow man. Man's spiritual unity must be to love creation, love his Creator, love everything that is created, and love his fellow man. A man that is spiritually united within himself is a man with inner peace. He is in favor with both God and man. He has an inner peace that is the essence of all happiness.[112]

If our trust and dependency are in anything or anyone other than Jesus and His Word, we are headed towards a life of hurt, frustration, and disappointment. All of the things that bring us happiness will soon vanish. All of the people we depend on will kick us to the curb. The little money we have will lose its value. Our health, if it has not already failed us, will fail us. The friends we thought we had will one day walk out of our lives.

What I am trying to say is that any and every thing other than Jesus and His Word is false security and has a guaranteed and unpredictable date of expiration. We cannot put our trust in what we see, hear, feel, touch, and smell. Those are our physical senses, and they are useless and destructive for the spiritual battles we face every day in this world.

Our trust should never be in people, things, or our senses. Our trust should be in Jesus Christ and nothing else. In all our ways, we should acknowledge Him. We should trust in the Lord with all our hearts and lean not to our understanding. To step toward our destiny, we must step away from our false

---

[112]Ibid, 233.

security. Being where God wants us to be requires our letting go of every pain, disappointment, failure, hurt, and fear.

Jesus wants us to know that all answers lie within Him and without Him we are weak, defeated, defenseless, helpless, hopeless, deceived, and powerless. We are living as an organization and not an organism; and destined to spend eternity in Hell. He is the Author and Finisher of our faith. Hebrews 12:2, "Looking unto Jesus the author and finisher of our faith; who for the joy that was set before him endured the cross, despising the shame, and is set down at the right hand of the throne of God."

Therefore, it is up to us to take action if we want to see progress and change in our homes, families, communities, churches, jobs, careers, children, marriages, and most importantly, our race. It can start by taking action with the recommendations addressed in Table 15.

TABLE 15 TAKING ACTION

No.	Take Action	Scripture Reference
1.	Walk in the power and authority that God has given to us.	2 Thessalonians 3:6
2.	Stop conforming to the ways of this world.	1 Peter 1:14
3.	Speak the Word to the enemy.	Jeremiah 23:28
4.	Let the enemy know who we are in Christ.	Ephesians 1:3
5.	Tell the enemy we know we are in covenant with the Living God.	Hebrews 9:15
6.	Live like Christians 24/7 at home, at work, and in our respective communities.	Galatians 2:14

12. MOVING FORWARD IN CHRIST

There comes a point in our lives when we must make a decision to deal with past hurts and pains, in addition to our problems, and press our way forward. As stated so plainly in Philippians 3:13-14, "Brethren, I count not myself to have apprehended: but this one thing I do, forgetting those things which are behind, and reaching forth unto those things which are before, [14] I press toward the mark for the prize of the high calling of God in Christ Jesus."

Without a doubt, problems are an often discussed and unresolved topic in African-American households. God is often trying to tell us something with the problems He permits in our lives. The problems we face will either defeat us or strengthen us, depending on how we respond to them. Unfortunately, most ~~black~~ people fail to consider how God wants to use problems for their good in their lives. We react foolishly, cry discrimination and resent our problems rather than pausing to consider what benefits we might bring by trusting and depending on God to bring us through the tests. Some of the tests we face are listed and described in Table 16.

TABLE 16 HOW GOD USES PROBLEMS

Test	Defined	Scripture
1.God uses problems to test us.	God will test us to see if we have the faith to trust Him and stand on His Word. In fact, God will be quiet while we take the test because He has already given us the answers.	Job 7:17-21 Psalms 139:23 Zechariah 13:7-9 1 Peter 4:12
2.God uses problems to direct us.	Sometimes God must light a fire under us to get us moving. Problems often point us in a new direction and motivate us to change.	Proverbs 20:30
3.God uses problems to inspect us.	People are like tea bags...If you want to know what is inside them, just drop them into hot water. When we have many kinds of troubles, we should be full of joy because we know that these troubles test our faith.	James 1:2-3
4 God uses problems to correct us.	Some lessons we learn only through pain and failure. Sometimes we only learn the value of something (health, money, a relationship, etc.) by losing it.	Psalms 119:71-72
5.God uses problems to protect us.	A problem can be a blessing in disguise if it prevents you from being hurt by something more serious.	Genesis 50:20
6.God uses problems to perfect us.	Problems, when responded to correctly, are character builders. God is far more interested in your character than your comfort.	Romans 5:3-4

There are problems that are designed to test, direct, inspect, correct, protect, promote, perfect, and boast about our faith in Him. If we do not pass the test, we cannot expect to move forward in Christ. God is not a professor. He does not grade on a curve. With God, it is pass or fail. However, when we do fail, we will take the test again. Nevertheless, when our tests are viewed from a biblical perspective, they provide the greatest opportunities to grow spiritually and become huge difference-makers.

It is time for the Black man to shake off the victim's robe of psychological oppression and put on the new robe called the "I" Factor. The "I" Factor is about what "I" can do to make the world a better place for the black race, for the black community and black manhood. It is time that the black man shakes off his robe of blaming and complaining and put on his new robe. The black man must realize that even if the white man is the cause of his sorrows, he is not the solution. The solution to the black man's problem is to take up the "I" Factor to do something to lift up his race, to do something to uplift his black community, and to do something to uplift black manhood. Let no black man say he is too weak to make himself a better person. Let no black man ever feel he is too angry to give a smile, to give a handshake, to lift up another brother. Let no black man think he is too poor or too feeble to wear the robe of the "I" Factor. Praise is the food of life, but who is to praise the black man if not another black man? However, self-praise results in malnutrition. The "I" Factor is the only defense for the black man against this spiritual dysfunction.[113]

Starting in slavery, it became necessary for the black man to find a comfort zone in the victim's coat, simply because

[113] Asher Ledwidge. *Saving the Black Culture A Revolution of Hope- Black Unity-Brotherly Love.* (Clermont, Florida: Self-published Asher Ledwidge; 2004), 17.

the coat was vital to his survival. Vital to suppress an appetite for hostile revenge. Vital to protect the wounds and cover all the scars inflicted by the cruel actions of oppression. Vital to nurture a false sense of inferiority that inflicts all oppressed people all over the world. In any relationship between victim and victimizer, the victim looks at the oppressor and makes of him not an unholy one, but a knight in shining shield and armor. This also places on the oppressor a false sense of superiority. The oppressor in the company of the wounded victim cherishes the feeling of his shining armor because it gives him an even greater illusion of superiority.[114]

The spiritual law of universal ones makes no exception. In all cases, it ties the victim to the victimizer. However, this time it is an unholy bonding. Call it the law of providence. When the law of providence works in this kind of unholy bonding, the victim offers the mantle of his own self-worth as his sacrifice at the altar in this unholy bonding and with each trip to the altar, this victim's coat gets thicker and longer. His victim's coat becomes his defense against oppression. We see the victim coming to the altar every day, offering his soul to the oppressor. However, what has become of the oppressor? The oppressor comes to the same altar in his suit of shield and shining armor to get his drops of blood bleeding from the victim's soul. Without it, his feelings of superiority will crumble. He comes standing tall in his shield and armor, but deep within him he has a trembling soul. A trembling soul in a shell of fears.[115]

At the same altar, all the happiness, joy, and inner peacefulness of love has been long gone. On one side, the victimizer: a trembling soul because he stands in defiance of love.

---

[114]Asher Ledwidge. *Saving the Black Culture A Revolution of Hope-Black Unity-Brotherly Love*. (Clermont, Florida: Self-published Asher Ledwidge; 2004), 31.

[115]Ibid, 32.

On the other side, the victim: a bleeding soul because he stands denied of love. Both stand in need of love, both need to be born again, to be refilled and be redeemed with love.[116]

Nevertheless, we have in front of us an opportunity to be a special people in the sight of God by overcoming adversity with the love of Christ and Deuteronomy 7 provides us with the scriptures to follow.

Deuteronomy 7:6-10
For thou art an holy people unto the Lord thy God: the Lord thy God hath chosen thee to be a special people unto himself, above all people that are upon the face of the earth. [7] The Lord did not set his love upon you, nor choose you, because ye were more in number than any people; for ye were the fewest of all people: [8] But because the Lord loved you, and because he would keep the oath which he had sworn unto your fathers, hath the Lord brought you out with a mighty hand, and redeemed you out of the house of bondmen, from the hand of Pharaoh king of Egypt. [9] Know therefore that the Lord thy God, he is God, the faithful God, which keepeth covenant and mercy with them that love him and keep his commandments to a thousand generations; [10] And repayeth them that hate him to their face, to destroy them: he will not be slack to him that hateth him, he will repay him to his face.

Regardless of our race, color, beliefs, and differences, God expects us to love one another to the point that we would lay down our life for the brethren. Nevertheless, we stand guilty of loving in word only. However, that is not what the scriptures tells us in 1 John 3.

[116]Ibid, 32.

1 John 3:16-18
Hereby perceive we the love of God, because he
laid down his life for us: and we ought to lay down
our lives for the brethren. [17] But whoso hath this
world's good, and seeth his brother have need, and
shutteth up his bowels of compassion from him, how
dwelleth the love of God in him? [18] My little children, let us not love in word, neither in tongue; but in
deed and in truth.

On the contrary, all relationships come with expectations.
Love and truth are two of those expectations. First, who in
their right mind goes into a relationship without expectations?
As a minimum, we expect truth and honesty, and that does not
mean very much without love and commitment. We should
praise God that we are in a relationship with a God who will
always love us, a God who has made a covenant with us that
He will never break. People enter into personal relationships
expecting and believing that they will receive something they
want or need. We have certain expectations from those we
have a relationship with, and we believe they can fulfill those
expectations. In fact, we stay in those relationships longer
than we should looking, hoping and believing we will eventually receive everything that was expected and promised.

Relationships are at the core of resolving many of the
issues we have in the black community. We cannot enter into
relationships to see what we can get out of a person and drop
them when we get what we want or keep them on speed dial
until we need them again for something else. God is a rela-
tional God and desires to have a committed relationship with
his children. He expected it from the beginning with Adam
and Eve and enjoyed it until sin separated them. Genesis
3:8, "And they heard the voice of the Lord God walking in
the garden in the cool of the day: and Adam and his wife hid

themselves from the presence of the Lord God amongst the trees of the garden."

Some of the common issues we face in the black community that can hinder our progress from moving forward and helping others are described in Table 17, Issues in the Black Community.

TABLE 17 ISSUES IN THE BLACK COMMUNITY[117]

No.	Issues and Concerns Facing the Black Community
1.	Is there a prejudice in black people against people of their race?
2.	Is there a lack of money; that is, do black people have enough money to spend? Or is it true the black economy in America is about equal to the third or fourth largest in the world?
3.	Does the service provided by black merchants at least equal the services given by other races? What about the prices in the black communities? What about the quality of the products? Can you find a good bargain from a black merchant?
4.	Is a black customer more polite to a white salesperson than to a black salesperson? Are black people too often unkind and impolite to each other?
5.	Does the black man of today have what it takes to run a successful small business or even a large one? Does he have the self-discipline? Is he willing to work the long hours of hard work, the hours of reading books about his business, the hours it may require to, for example, fix cars or put on a roof in the daytime, then come home at night and do two or three more hours of book work?

[117]Asher Ledwidge. Saving the Black Culture A Revolution of Hope-Black Unity-Brotherly Love. (Clermont, Florida: Self-published Asher Ledwidge; 2004), 21.

No.	Issues and Concerns Facing the Black Community
6.	Does the black man of today have the strong support, love and harmony within his family necessary to succeed in any small business? It seems wherever you see a small business running well, it is always a family affair or else a partnership affair.
7.	Could it be that the black man's feelings of being alone are not good for business? If you look at small businesses of all the other races, you will surely see that most are family affairs.
8.	Should a black person ignore prices, the quality of products and the quality of services in order to support a business just because it is a black business?
9.	Is the black man ready, willing and able to look inside himself for answers?

Regardless of all of the issues and concerns addressed in Table 19, Issues and Concerns Facing the Black Community, we should never allow our minds to entertain the thought that we can sit in the presence of God with needs that would be ignored by a Father who loves us and wants to bless us. His Word expresses His love for us in Luke 11.

Luke 11:11-13
If a son shall ask bread of any of you that is a father, will he give him a stone? or if he ask a fish, will he for a fish give him a serpent? [12] Or if he shall ask an egg, will he offer him a scorpion? [13] If ye then, being evil, know how to give good gifts unto your children: how much more shall your heavenly Father give the Holy Spirit to them that ask him?

Our earthly father's resources are limited and our relationship and dependence on him is only for a season. However, our heavenly Father has unlimited resources and our relationship with Him never ends. As a result, we have the opportunity to move forward in Christ and become Kingdom men for the Kingdom of God. Nonetheless, a large portion of black men's manhood has been forfeited simply because they do not understand or live according to the theological perspective on what it means to be a Kingdom man. Man's false definitions of manhood exist, including the following in Table 18, False Definitions of Manhood.[118]

TABLE 18 FALSE DEFINITIONS OF MANHOOD

No.	Type of Man	Definition
1.	Passive Man	A male who is unable or unwilling to take the leadership role that God has assigned him to have.
2.	Domineering Man	A male who thinks manhood is measured by his ability to emotionally and /or physically force compliance to his demands.
3.	Sexual Man	A male who measures his manhood by the amount of women he can conquer.
4.	Corporate Man	A male who defines his manhood by the amount of time he invests in this career and / or by the amount of money he can accrue.
5.	Irresponsible Man	A male who refuses to provide properly for the well-being of those around him.
6.	Hedonistic Man	A male who lives for self-gratifying pleasure at the expense of those around him.

[118]Tony Evans. *Kingdom Man*. (Carol Stream, Illinois: Tyndale House Publishers, Inc.; 2012), 59.

Only when a man functions as a biblical kingdom man will he experience the fullness of his destiny. Yet when a man does not live according to the biblical definition of manhood, it shows up in his own life and in the lives under his influence and care. Many men are out of alignment with God, because they have gotten their definition of manhood from illegitimate, inadequate, or errant sources including the media, male influences in their life, the home they grew up in, or even music. However, there is more to being a man than what these sources may say. Being a Kingdom man involves exercising authority and responsibility along with wisdom and compassion. A Kingdom man intentionally aligns his life, choices, thoughts, and actions under the lordship of Jesus Christ.[119]

Without a doubt, we must align our lives under the Lordship of Jesus, knowing that God does not change, His Word does not change, and neither do His basic expectations for believers. God the Father, the Son, and the Holy Spirit still expects us to be holy, to walk in the light, to walk by faith, to preach and teach His Word, to win lost souls, and to love and forgive with the love of Christ.

However, God's personal expectations for all of us do change as we grow spiritually and mature in our relationship with Him. He requires more of us as we do more for the Kingdom of God. Yet, when we consistently begin to do more for the Lord, the enemy begins to fear the Christ in us. On the other hand, when we do less or nothing for Christ, the enemy will make sure that we do not move forward. Besides, we are on the verge of putting the devil in the unemployment line because we are not doing enough for the Kingdom of God that concerns him enough to come after us. As Christians who desire to move forward, we need to be informed every now and then that the God we serve is a jealous God. The

---

[119]Tony Evans. *Kingdom Man*. (Carol Stream, Illinois: Tyndale House Publishers, Inc.; 2012), 61.

book of Nahum explains God's jealousy within the following scriptures.

Nahum 1:2-7
God is jealous, and the Lord revengeth; the Lord revengeth, and is furious; the Lord will take vengeance on his adversaries, and he reserveth wrath for his enemies. [3] The Lord is slow to anger, and great in power, and will not at all acquit the wicked: the Lord hath his way in the whirlwind and in the storm, and the clouds are the dust of his feet. [4] He rebuketh the sea, and maketh it dry, and drieth up all the rivers: Bashan languisheth, and Carmel, and the flower of Lebanon languisheth. [5] The mountains quake at him, and the hills melt, and the earth is burned at his presence, yea, the world, and all that dwell therein. [6] Who can stand before his indignation? and who can abide in the fierceness of his anger? his fury is poured out like fire, and the rocks are thrown down by him. [7] The Lord is good, a strong hold in the day of trouble; and he knoweth them that trust in him.

For the same reason, Jesus loved us so much that He wrote 66 books for us called the Bible, the inspired Word of God. It was written by 40 different authors with a variety of backgrounds (shepherds, fishermen, doctors, kings, prophets and others), most of whom never personally knew one another. It was written in three different languages: Hebrew, Greek, and Aramaic. It was written on three different continents — Africa, Asia, and Europe — with no errors and no contradictions. All 66 books share a common storyline: the creation, fall, and redemption of God's people. They also share a common theme: Salvation is available to whoever repents of his sin and accepts Jesus in his heart as Lord of his life.

That is to say, the Word of God has all of the instructions we need to move forward in Christ with the ability to prosper. In accordance with the Word spoken in Joshua 1:8, "This book of the law shall not depart out of thy mouth; but thou shalt meditate therein day and night, that thou mayest observe to do according to all that is written therein: for then thou shalt make thy way prosperous, and then thou shalt have good success."

To summarize, we need a Pentecostal experience to position the African-American race to move forward in unity as one with all races in Christ as witnessed in Acts 2. We need to be filled with the Holy Spirit and walk in unity under the direction of the Holy Spirit. We do not need leaders who are not following Christ and living according to the Word of God.

Acts 2:1-21
And when the day of Pentecost was fully come, they were all with one accord in one place. [2] And suddenly there came a sound from heaven as of a rushing mighty wind, and it filled all the house where they were sitting. [3] And there appeared unto them cloven tongues like as of fire, and it sat upon each of them. [4] And they were all filled with the Holy Ghost, and began to speak with other tongues, as the Spirit gave them utterance. [5] And there were dwelling at Jerusalem Jews, devout men, out of every nation under heaven. [6] Now when this was noised abroad, the multitude came together, and were confounded, because that every man heard them speak in his own language. [7] And they were all amazed and marvelled, saying one to another, Behold, are not all these which speak Galilaeans? [8] And how hear we every man in our own tongue, wherein we were born? [9] Parthians, and Medes, and Elamites, and the dwellers in Mesopotamia, and in Judaea, and Cappadocia, in

Pontus, and Asia, [10] Phrygia, and Pamphylia, in Egypt, and in the parts of Libya about Cyrene, and strangers of Rome, Jews and proselytes, [11] Cretes and Arabians, we do hear them speak in our tongues the wonderful works of God. [12] And they were all amazed, and were in doubt, saying one to another, What meaneth this? [13] Others mocking said, These men are full of new wine. [14] But Peter, standing up with the eleven, lifted up his voice, and said unto them, Ye men of Judaea, and all ye that dwell at Jerusalem, be this known unto you, and hearken to my words: [15] For these are not drunken, as ye suppose, seeing it is but the third hour of the day. [16] But this is that which was spoken by the prophet Joel; [17] And it shall come to pass in the last days, saith God, I will pour out of my Spirit upon all flesh: and your sons and your daughters shall prophesy, and your young men shall see visions, and your old men shall dream dreams: [18] And on my servants and on my handmaidens I will pour out in those days of my Spirit; and they shall prophesy: [19] And I will shew wonders in heaven above, and signs in the earth beneath; blood, and fire, and vapour of smoke: [20] The sun shall be turned into darkness, and the moon into blood, before that great and notable day of the Lord come: [21] And it shall come to pass, that whosoever shall call on the name of the Lord shall be saved.

✳ Finally, when we experience adversity, we generally respond in one of three ways: (1) we become angry; (2) we try to gut it out; or (3) we accept it with joy. No one makes it through life without adversities; we all have issues. However, we all have a free will to choose how to move forward. Table 19 explains our adversity experiences and choices.

TABLE 19 EXPERIENCING ADVERSITY[120]

No.	Adversity	Response
1.	Anger	When adversity comes our way, we say, "Why me, Lord?" We become bitter and resentful and blame God and others for our problems. We view ourselves as victims and demand that God answer our accusing questions: "Why don't You love me, Lord?" We feel entitled to life, health, wealth, and happiness.
2.	Gutting it Out	Another way we respond to adversity is by adopting a stoic attitude, repressing our emotions. We lie to ourselves and say, "I'm gutting it out. I'm demonstrating endurance." In reality, we are merely isolating ourselves with a shell of false bravado. We do not meditate on God's love, we do not pray, we do not believe God has anything good planned for us. We simply tell ourselves, "This will soon be over. I'm a survivor." We never receive what God has planned for us if we stay here.
3.	Accepting it With Joy	Joy is the response God seeks from us. When adversity comes, we rest in His love and trust that He knows best. We realize that nothing can happen to us without His permission. If there is pain in our lives, we know it is because God deems it necessary for our growth or wishes to use our pain to minister to others. God revealed to the prophet Habakkuk that the Babylonians would invade Israel. Habakkuk knew that Israel was about to suffer intense adversity as part of God's loving discipline of His people. Habakkuk faced the looming national tragedy with an attitude of acceptance with joy.

[120]www.crosswalkmail.com/
mcdbqscdbwblcpdkltgvzlmzcslpyggpwnczqqktwwynsts_thbvhzblclph.html

If Habakkuk could be joyful in the face of a national calamity, then we, the ~~African American~~ race should be able to rejoice in the Lord, no matter what comes our way.

13. HEALING AND RESTORATION

E very African-American adult and child in our society today, in truth, has lost some or a vital part of his spiritual holiness because of his or her worldly challenges and decisions. Nevertheless, every one of us should actively seek the face of God for spiritual redemption.

Man may seek many different paths to his redemption, but only when he follows a spiritual path will he be redeemed. The black man, like every other man, needs to wake up every day singing the redemption song. The black man's road to his redemption has longer paths of loneliness and is covered with more dark clouds. Slavery, colonialism and racism have left a unique brand of sorrow on the Black man's soul. These three demons not only haunt him, but also put a curse on the whole human race. Today, the black man remains the victim of the effects of these three demons. It is important to note that the black man was not always the victim of slavery, colonialism and racism. Long ago, back in Egypt, black men were the slave masters and the victimizers.[121]

---

[121] Asher Ledwidge. *For The Black Man Soul And Redemption Promoting Black Manhood. Guide to Maintaining a Delicate Balance between Material Consumption and Spiritual Fulfillment.* (Clermont, Florida: Nuf-Love Publications; 2001), 131.

Every system of victims and victimizers has the upper hand because many victims and victimizers walk on separate grounds. However, every black man can feel good in knowing that the road to redemption is only one road going in only one direction. From Jesus to Martin Luther King, Jr. to Gandhi, they all preached that the road to redemption could only be traveled with brotherly love. Redemption means the victim must learn to love and forgive, and the victimizer must learn to love. The victimizer has long lost his inner peace and capacity for love, and he seeks to take away the inner peace and spiritual holiness of his victims. However, the power of love is not given by man, and man can only take away one's spiritual wholeness when one chooses to let him have it.[122]

Admittedly, the bonding between the white man and the black man is shattered. Who is to blame? All of society is suffering from the pain of pieces of broken glass lying on the floor on the road to a righteous redemption. It would seem that the righteous thing to do would be for the white man and the black man to join in love and harmony; laboring together to pick up the pieces of broken glass, making the pathway smooth and safe on the road to a unified redemption of black and white. The road to redemption must be a walk and not a talk. The road to redemption must be a place of inner stillness and peacefulness. Learning to walk by faith and not by sight is redemptive. The soul rejoices in the spiritual light of holiness.[123]

Without a doubt, redemption comes from the hand of God. Man does not possess redeeming grace; it is a gift from God

---

[122]Asher Ledwidge. *For The Black Man Soul And Redemption Promoting Black Manhood. Guide to Maintaining a Delicate Balance between Material Consumption and Spiritual Fulfillment.* (Clermont, Florida: Nuf-Love Publications; 2001), 134.

[123]Ibid, 135.

alone, for the people of God. The same restoration power that God extended to Joel is available for His people today.

Joel 2:25-27
And I will restore to you the years that the locust hath eaten, the cankerworm, and the caterpillar, and the palmerworm, my great army which I sent among you. [26] And ye shall eat in plenty, and be satisfied, and praise the name of the LORD your God, that hath dealt wondrously with you: and my people shall never be ashamed. [27] And ye shall know that I am in the midst of Israel and that I am the LORD your God and none else: and my people shall never be ashamed.

Prayer is for the healing and restoration in the black community. It is not about establishing a pattern of daily prayers that eventually becomes religious and an opportunity to check a box to say, "We have prayed every day." Prayer is about establishing a season and a lifestyle of prayer, where prayer becomes a continuous and constant part of whom and what we are in Christ. It is through prayer that we establish a relationship with the Lord and receive His divine direction and guidance to proceed forward in our healing and restoration.

Furthermore, the scriptures are unfaultable; we do not know what to pray for unless the Holy Spirit leads us through intercession. Romans 8:26-27, "Likewise the Spirit also helpeth our infirmities: for we know not what we should pray for as we ought: but the Spirit itself maketh intercession for us with groanings which cannot be uttered. [27] And he that searcheth the hearts knoweth what is the mind of the Spirit, because he maketh intercession for the saints according to the will of God." There are times in our lives we have to break away from our prayer partners and find a place to pray alone and cry out to God. Cry out to God to heal and restore things in us that we are too embarrassed to share with others. Just as

Jesus required quality time with God as seen in Mark 6:45-46, "And straightway he constrained his disciples to get into the ship, and to go to the other side before unto Bethsaida, while he sent away the people. [46] And when he had sent them away, he departed into a mountain to pray."

As wounded and fragile warriors for Christ, some of the greatest challenges in our prayers is waiting, listening, and receiving what we have heard in our spirit. Unfortunately, patience is a virtue that is often missing from African-Americans due to the long history of waiting and praying for change. Nevertheless, what a blessing it is to do as Psalm 27:14 has instructed us, "Wait on the Lord: be of good courage, and he shall strengthen thine heart: wait, I say, on the Lord." We need to be taught how to wait in a world that wants everything right now.

Once we develop a seasonal prayer life, we will find ourselves constantly seeking God for His divine direction and purpose in our lives. We will learn how to trust, wait, and listen for the voice of God according to Proverbs 3:5-6, "Trust in the Lord with all thine heart; and lean not unto thine own understanding. [6] In all thy ways acknowledge him, and he shall direct thy paths." These two verses of scripture are powerful and instrumental to our life of seasonal prayer. However, we must also remember that there will be situations in our lives that will require us to spend the night with God in all night prayer, just like Jesus did in Luke 6:12, "And it came to pass in those days, that he went out into a mountain to pray, and continued all night in prayer to God. It is through continued prayer that God qualifies the unqualified to do the impossible. Not only is prayer critical to our healing process, we need to lie before God and cry out for Him to put away our bitterness, anger, un-forgiveness, and disobedience. Table 20, Prayers that Bring Healing, is a good place to start.

TABLE 20 PRAYERS THAT BRING HEALING[124]

No.	By Putting Away Bitterness	By Putting Away Anger	By Putting Away Unforgiveness	Through Obedience
1.	Lord, I give the bitterness of my soul to you. Please look upon my affliction and remember me. I will go in peace because you have granted my petition.	I will cease from anger and put away wrath to stay connected to God.	I will go to my brother and ask that he forgive me of my trespasses against him.	I will obey the voice of my Father, according to all He has commanded me.
2.	I will speak openly to you, O Lord, and release all of my bitterness to you.	I will speak soft words, kind words, and words of life to turn wrath and anger away from me. I will not grieve anyone with my words.	I pray that my brother will forgive me, so that when I go before God, He will take this death away from me.	I will obey the voice of the angel of the Lord to keep me in the right way and bring me to a place that God Himself has prepared for me.
3.	I declare that I will not die in the bitterness of my soul, and I will eat with pleasure.	I will appease the strife against my health and my family by being slow to anger.	Like Moses, I come to you asking Your forgiveness on behalf of Your people and myself.	As I obey the angel of the Lord and do all that God has spoken through him, my enemies will be God's enemies.

---

[124]John Eckhardt, *Prayers that Bring Healing*. Lake Mary, Florida: (Charisma House; 2010), 14-15, 23-32, 36, 38-41.

No.	By Putting Away Bitterness	By Putting Away Anger	By Putting Away Unforgiveness	Through Obedience
4.	I will raise wise children who will cause me no grief or bitterness.	I am better than the mighty, because I control my anger. There is more gain in ruling my spirit than in conquering a city.	With Jesus, I pray, "Father, forgive them, for they do not know what they do."	I obey the voice of the Lord, for He is my life, and in Him is the length of days.
5.	I had great bitterness, but in love, You delivered me from the pit of corruption. For You have put all my sins behind Your back.	I use discretion to defer my anger; I earn esteem by overlooking wrongs.	Forgive me of my sins, and have compassion upon me.	Let me not be like those who obey unrighteousness, indignation, and wrath, for tribulation and anguish are their portions.
6.	I was in bitterness and the heat of my spirit, but the hand of the Lord is strong upon me.	I declare that anger's reign in my life will come to an end.	O Lord, hear. O Lord, forgive. O Lord, listen and do! For I am called by Your name.	I will not be like the fathers of Israel. I will humble and submit to obeying the Lord. I will be mindful of the wonders that God does on my behalf, for He is gracious and merciful, ready to pardon, slow to anger, and of great kindness. He has not forsaken me.

No.	By Putting Away Bitterness	By Putting Away Anger	By Putting Away Unforgiveness	Through Obedience
7.	I repent of my wickedness and pray to God that the thoughts of my heart be forgiven, for I am bound by bitterness and iniquity.	I cast out cruelty and destruction of wrath and anger. They will not flood my emotions any longer.	Like the servant who owed the king ten thousand talents, I too have been forgiven much. Therefore, I will go and forgive all those who have sinned against me so that I will not be given over to the tormentors.	I will spend my days in prosperity and my years in pleasure. I will not perish and die without knowledge because I obey and serve the Lord.
8.	My mouth is full of cursing and bitterness, but You have shown me a better way, and I have been made right in Your sight.	Let all wrath and anger be put away from me.	If I forgive others, I will be forgiven.	I will amend my ways and my doings. I will obey the voice of the Lord my God, and the Lord will relinquish the evil that He had pronounced against me.
9.	I diligently look within myself so that I will not be defiled by any root of bitterness that may spring up.	I am a new person, having been renewed after the image of Him who created me; therefore, I put off anger.	Forgive me of my sins because I also have forgiven all those whom I felt were indebted to me. Keep me from temptation, and deliver me from evil.	I will obey Your voice, and You will be my God. I will walk in all the ways that You have commanded me, and it will be well with me.

No.	By Putting Away Bitterness	By Putting Away Anger	By Putting Away Unforgiveness	Through Obedience
10.	My heart knows its bitterness; I release it to you.	I will not discourage my children by provoking them to anger.	I declare that Satan will not get an advantage over me because I walk in forgiveness just as Christ did. I am not ignorant of the devil's devices.	Whether I like or not, I will obey the voice of the Lord my God, that it may be well with me.

We have a Father who has instructed us to ask Him for the things we need in accordance with Matthew 7.

Matthew 7:7-11
Ask, and it shall be given you; seek, and ye shall find; knock, and it shall be opened unto you: |8| For every one that asketh receiveth; and he that seeketh findeth; and to him that knocketh it shall be opened. |9| Or what man is there of you, whom if his son ask bread, will he give him a stone? |10| Or if he ask a fish, will he give him a serpent? |11| If ye then, being evil, know how to give good gifts unto your children, how much more shall your Father which is in heaven give good things to them that ask him?

The blessings of the Lord are for the "now" and the "when." As Christians, our excitement and joy for the "when" far exceeds our excitement and joy for the "now." The "when" is when we get to Heaven and the "now" is right now, the life we are currently living right here and right now. However, we have to learn to overcome the attacks against us by the enemy as described in Table 21, Attacks from the Enemy to enjoy the "now."

TABLE 21 ATTACKS FROM THE ENEMY

No.	Area Attacked	Scriptures
1	Body (Health)	Psalms 107:20–He sent his word, and healed them, and delivered them from their destructions.
2	Finances (poverty)	Deuteronomy 8:18-19–But thou shalt remember the LORD thy God: for it is he that giveth thee power to get wealth, that he may establish his covenant which he sware unto thy fathers, as it is this day. [19] And it shall be, if thou do at all forget the LORD thy God, and walk after other gods, and serve them, and worship them, I testify against you this day that ye shall surely perish.
3	Relationships (our love for one another)	Romans 5:5–And hope maketh not ashamed; because the love of God is shed abroad in our hearts by the Holy Ghost which is given unto us.
4	The Mind	Philippians 4:8–Finally, brethren, whatsoever things are true, whatsoever things are honest, whatsoever things are just, whatsoever things are pure, whatsoever things are lovely, whatsoever things are of good report; if there be any virtue, and if there be any praise, think on these things.

Part of our healing and restoration is in God's grace. His grace was a gift that was given; it cannot be earned or merited by what we do and do not do. It requires faith to receive the grace that God has for us as described in Galatians 5.

Galatians 5:1-6
Stand fast therefore in the liberty wherewith Christ hath made us free, and be not entangled again with the yoke of bondage. [2] Behold, I Paul say unto you, that if ye be circumcised, Christ shall profit you nothing. [3] For I testify again to every man that is circumcised, that he is a debtor to do the whole law. [4] Christ is become of no effect unto you , whosoever of you are justified by the law; ye are fallen from grace. [5] For we through the Spirit wait for the hope of righteousness by faith.[6] For in Jesus Christ neither circumcision availeth any thing, nor uncircumcision; but faith which worketh by love.

Falling from grace means that we try to merit God's favor and love by our own works. Many think that not trying hard to please God is falling from grace but in fact, it is the opposite. "Falling from grace" is used once in the scriptures and refers to "trying to gain or maintain your righteousness." Falling from grace is not the loss of salvation. It is a practical reality that means you do not receive God's grace in your life because you are trying to earn a gift, you are too busy working to stop, rest, and receive Christ's gift. When you have fallen from grace, it is not because you have done something wrong, but because you are not receiving God's grace in your relationship with Him.[125]

---

[125]http://love-god-love-others.blogspot.com/2012/03/meaning-of-fallen-from-grace.html

We nullify the grace of God when we try to be good on our own. It is not that His favor for us ends; it is that we live as though His favor/grace does not make us right with Him (justified or righteous), so we try to earn God's favor by doing for God instead of trusting in God. Law (principles, rules, requirements, and expectations) points you to yourself and your efforts. Grace points you to Christ and His efforts on your behalf.[126]

It is sad that almost 100% of how Christianity is preached and taught is to live in that fallen from grace state; that everything depends on you, and if you mess up you are separated from fellowship with God and you have to strive to do great things for God.

Those things sound good and right. However, God's ways are far above our ways. We do not have to earn God's favor to be saved; nor do we have to earn it to continue in life. We have it. We do not have to earn God's approval by what we do any more than an infant has to earn his or her parents' approval.[127]

On the other hand, for those of us who may have been misinformed to believe we have fallen from grace — it is not true; release the guilt. We will know if this describes us because our confidence will have switched from what Jesus has done to what we are doing. The peace and the joy that we once knew will be replaced by fear, anxiety, and condemnation day after day. Why? Because whatever we are doing can never measure up to the righteous requirements of the law. In fact, we cannot measure up to our standards.

Everything we do calls for love in one way or another. However, there are three different branches of love — soulful, narcissistic, and material — that are the cause of the civil war in every man, as shown in Figure 19, The Trinity of Love.

---

[126]Ibid

[127]http://love-god-love-others.blogspot.com/2012/03/meaning-of-fallen-from-grace.html

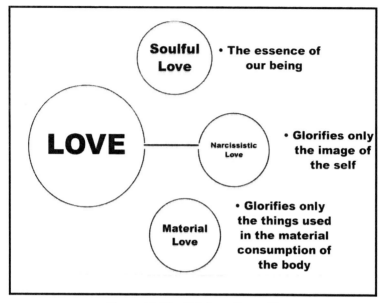

Figure 19. The Trinity of Love.[128]

Similarly, we have a battle on our hands to reach the point where we can easily do the things we desire to do in our spirit. As much as we may want to please God and deny our flesh to reach that pinnacle area of healing and restoration, it will be a struggle. Not just a one-time struggle, but a constant struggle within; but God knows our heart and according to Romans 7, the struggle is expected.

Romans 7:13-25
Was then that which is good made death unto me? God forbid. But sin, that it might appear sin, working death in me by that which is good; that sin by the

---

[128]Asher Ledwidge. *Saving the Black Culture A Revolution of Hope-Black Unity-Brotherly Love*. (Clermont, Florida: Self-published Asher Ledwidge; 2004), 236.

commandment might become exceeding sinful. [14] For we know that the law is spiritual: but I am carnal, sold under sin. [15] For that which I do I allow not: for what I would, that do I not; but what I hate, that do I. [16] If then I do that which I would not, I consent unto the law that it is good. [17] Now then it is no more I that do it, but sin that dwelleth in me. [18] For I know that in me (that is, in my flesh,) dwelleth no good thing: for to will is present with me; but how to perform that which is good I find not. [19] For the good that I would I do not: but the evil which I would not, that I do. [20] Now if I do that I would not, it is no more I that do it, but sin that dwelleth in me. [21] I find then a law, that, when I would do good, evil is present with me. [22] For I delight in the law of God after the inward man: [23] But I see another law in my members, warring against the law of my mind, and bringing me into captivity to the law of sin which is in my members. [24] O wretched man that I am! who shall deliver me from the body of this death? [25] I thank God through Jesus Christ our Lord. So then with the mind I myself serve the law of God; but with the flesh the law of sin.

The inner peace and harmony of a unified self will always lead to the unity and harmony of the black family. A man at peace with himself is better able to be a loving father, a loving husband and a loving brother. Unification of all black families will never happen until we as a people can reverse the breakup of black families caused by slavery. Our society of materialism only gives lip service to the spiritual integrity of families. A person with no family love is a person in the grip of fear, anger and self-doubt. Fear, anger and self-doubt certainly do not help build a unified nation. Unified families start with plenty of love within the family.

A man and woman who love each other romantically take the first step towards a unified family. Parental love will unify a family, with mothers and fathers loving and disciplining their children. Brotherly love is also important; brothers and sisters, aunts and uncles, grandparents, in-laws and cousins, all loving and showing full respect for each other. These are the building blocks of strong families, and strong families are the only way to build a strong and unified nation.[129]

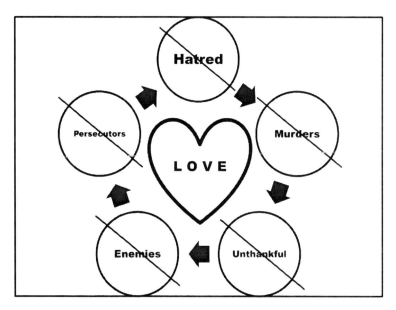

Figure 20. The Cancellation Power of True Love.

[129]Asher Ledwidge. *Saving the Black Culture A Revolution of Hope-Black Unity-Brotherly Love*. (Clermont, Florida: Self-published Asher Ledwidge; 2004), 239.

Furthermore, the power of love that we are capable of releasing into an environment of hatred, murders, persecutors, enemies, and un-thankfulness is a great spiritual prescription. Love has the power to cancel all of the adversities that man can launch in our direction. The power of that love as shown in Figure 20, The Cancellation Power of True Love.

In the same way, the healing and restoration for the African-American family and community can be easily summarized with a song of redemption that touches every struggle, battle, and victory the African-American community has had to endure for hundreds of years. Now the recipe for life and the road to freedom lies in front of us as passionately stated in a "Song of Redemption."

A Song of Redemption[130]
My children, my children of Grace, you're gonna have to start the family over. It's on to you to set things straight. Y'all done traded one slavery from another when you turned your back on wisdom. You ain't free to do what you want to do; you free to do what you supposed to do. Find out what you're here for, what you were sent for.

Take care of children. Just 'cause they don't come from you don't mean they don't belong to you. Come back to truth. Tell others that they can't hate their masters and want to be like him. Tell them all they did when they were slaves. How they worked together and take care of one another. Tell them all they do with nothing and how they make everything work for somebody else. They can learn their history. Tell them to love, to forgive, to never forget.

---

[130]Bertice Berry. *The Ties That Bind*. (New York: The Doubleday Publishing Group; 2009), 173.

They have to stand ground 'cause bigger change than they see is coming. You the beginning of that change, but be careful. Change never comes without struggle, and joy never comes without pain.

In your lifetime, you will see a big struggle, but you have each other to get through it.

Don't let the little things keep you from doing the big things. Others will try to stop you, but things are already moving; they can't be stopped. Everybody who looks like you are not on your side. And everybody who don't, ain't against you.

Talk to God and never stop loving. The more I write, the more I see, the more I see, the more I know everything is gonna be okay. I can feel it. I'm leaving these papers right here cause I know they gonna find you.

It's my time, and I feel that, too. Learn from the past that's yours. Take the gift of what I done seen and use it to love. This is the Recipe of Life; the road to freedom. Freedom ain't just about living free it's about being free. The chains on our wrists ain't as strong as the chains on our mind. The only thing that can win over that evil is love. So learn to love, strive to love, 'cause we ain't got time for nothing else.

14. CONCLUSION

As African-Americans, we have to break the bad habit of blaming others for what has happened to us in the past and for things we were not personally able to accomplish. It is time to put our past in the right place, the past, and bury it. When we become mature enough to bury our past, we can see the reality of truth being processed through our minds. That is when our eyes will open to see that the major cause for our inconsistent progress is our lack of effort. I know there are exceptions, but I am not addressing the exceptions. I am addressing the major players of the "Blame Game," a game that has gotten old and predictable.

I know that many of my African-American brothers and sisters continue to blame the white race. However, it is no longer the white race or any other race that is holding us back or stopping us from achieving the success in life we desire. Our failures today are the product of our poor choices. We have become our greatest enemy. As African-Americans, we have to understand that our dreams and visions to have *this* and *that* and to be *this* and *that* are good; however, those dreams and visions require hard work, dedication, commitment, and goals.

Please understand that all African-Americans have a critical part in the healing and restoration of the African-American family. Regardless of our success, accomplishments, positions, titles, economical status, degrees, or age, we are not exempt from the success or failures of our race. If at any time, we choose to take a close look at ourselves, we will discover that there is always something we can do to help the cause.

There is a quote frequently used by Omega men, an African-American fraternity that says, "Excuses are tools of incompetence, that build monuments to nothing, and those who specialize in them, are seldom good at anything else." In other words, as long as we continue to make excuses for everything that we do not have and for everything that we cannot accomplish, we are building a negative memorial that can only hinder our progress.

Excuses are an avoidance of facts and accountability. For those of us who are parents, there is accountability and there are questions we need to address when it comes to raising our children in the society that we live in today. Like it or not, we are accountable for the behavior and choices our children make. We can no longer be hypocrites and tell them to "do as we say and not as we do;" that is a well-defined and unquestionable definition of a hypocrite. In other words, it is time to lead by example and not by words. Table 22 represents a series of check-in questions, an assessment that can change the relationship between African-American parents and their children.

TABLE 22 PARENTS' CHECK-IN QUESTIONS[131]

No.	Parent's Check-in Questions
1.	What is one thing I could show my children that demonstrates I have the power to improve myself?
2.	Does my child demonstrate a quality that I see in myself: easily frustrated, judgmental, short-tempered? How might I begin to make changes in this area?
3.	Who modeled anger for me as a child? Am I reflecting that way of expressing anger to my kids?
4.	What strong beliefs do I have? What about important values? Am I reflecting them well?
5.	Who and what am I using for my support system? Am I drawing on my spirituality and my religious beliefs for strength? If not, why not?
6.	Is there a spiritual practice or philosophy I would like to know more about: fasting, retreats, tithing, or journaling? Where can I begin?

At the same time, there are economic challenges and differences in income for African-American families that have not drastically improved over the years. The median household income in metropolitan regions by race and Hispanic origin (adjusted to 2009 in dollars) is shown in Table 23 and is documented by race. The gaps are not small by any standard. The bad news for African-Americans is that the gap is growing, year after year.

[131]Mimi Doe and Marsha Walch. *10 Principles for Spiritual Parenting.* (New York, NY: Harper Collins Publishers, Inc.; 1998), 288.

TABLE 23 MEDIAN HOUSEHOLD INCOME IN METROPOLITAN
REGIONS BY RACE[132]

Race and Hispanic Origin	1990	2000	2005-2009
Non-Hispanic White	$56,240	$62,066	$61,706
Black	**$34,496**	**$39,056**	**$37,047**
Black ratio to White	0.613	0.629	0.600
White-Black difference	**$21,745**	**$23,010**	**$24,659**
Hispanic	$40,566	$43,509	$42,098
Hispanic ratio to White	0.721	0.701	0.682
White-Hispanic difference	$15,675	$18,557	$19,609
Asian	$60,974	$66,822	$70,568
Asian ratio to White	1.084	1.077	1.144
White-Asian difference	-$4,734	-$4,756	-$8,862

Indeed, the gap is steadily increasing; however, when we begin to invest in our young African-American families through education, mentoring, love, and time, we can make a difference in the numbers — they can get better. If young

[132]http://www.s4.brown.edu/us2010/Data/Report/report0727.pdf

girls, at an early age, can plan to have babies and receive welfare checks, they can plan to become teachers, doctors, lawyers, entrepreneurs, and professionals. However, it will require a major change in their mindsets and their environments. Honestly, if young men can sell millions of dollars of drugs in their communities to people who are just as broke as they are, they can use those same sales and marketing skills to sell legal products for corporate America and change their lives and their communities.

Everything boils down to a choice. I am a product of the "hood," but I chose a better life for me and my family and stepped out on faith. However, faith without works is dead. It required working 40 hours a week while carrying a full load of classes each semester in college. It was a commitment that required attending school four nights a week and Saturday mornings. My parents called it "sacrifice." Nevertheless, it resulted in a college degree with honors. It opened doors for me in corporate America, doors that would never have been open for me if I had chosen to play "the Blame Game" and have a pity party about what I did not have.

On the other hand, we have a serious crime issue to address in the black communities. NAACP president Benjamin Jealous said that the verdict in the George Zimmerman case is a sign that African-Americans face "times of great peril." However, if there is a peril, Mr. Jealous should look our African-American communities for the cause. Most of the time when a murder victim is black, the perpetrator is not a white man; it is a black man, as reflected in the statistics in Table 24.[133]

---

[133]http://rare.us/story/white-on-black-murder-who-really-is-killing-whom/

TABLE 24 MURDERS BY RACE

Race of Victim	Total	Race of Offender			
		White	Black	Other	Unknown
White	3,172	2,630	448	33	61
Black	2,695	193	2,447	9	46
Other Race	180	45	36	99	0
Unknown Race	84	36	27	3	18

Without a doubt, we focus on our defeats and not our victories. We have to begin to focus more on our victories than our defeats. As African-Americans, we have battle after battle, but that does not mean God will not give us the victory if we consult Him and allow Him to fight our battles. When Joshua and the Israelites entered the Promised Land, they fought many battles. In fact, they fought 39 battles in the Promised Land compared to only two in their exodus from Egypt. God gave them the victory as long as they inquired of God. God will do the same for us because He is not a respecter of persons. We have had major milestones and victories throughout our history, and they should serve as motivation for the next one and the next one. Table 25 lists some of the most significant victories African-Americans have achieved during my lifetime.

TABLE 25 MAJOR AFRICAN-AMERICAN VICTORIES

No.	Major Milestone / Victory	Comments
1.	1954. "Brown decision" ending legal segregation.	May 17, 1954, the Supreme Court, in the case of Brown versus the Board of Education of Topeka, ended federally sanctioned racial segregation in public schools by ruling unanimously "separate educational facilities were inherently unequal."
2.	1961. Affirmative Action introduced.	President John F. Kennedy introduced the concept of affirmative action broadly across the United States with his Executive Order number 10925.
3.	1962. James Meredith enters the University of Mississippi, ending the state's defiance of federal law.	James Meredith had to be escorted by 127 Deputy Marshal federal troops to enter the University of Mississippi.
4.	1963. 250,000 people participate in the 1963 March on Washington, the biggest civil rights demonstration ever.	Washington, D.C. is where Dr. Martin Luther King, Jr. delivered his famous speech "I Have a Dream."
5.	1964. President Lyndon B. Johnson signs Economic Opportunity Act Civil Rights Bill.	The Economic Opportunity Act initiated the "war on poverty;" a Civil Rights Bill with public accommodations and fair employment sections.

No.	Major Milestone / Victory	Comments
6.	1964. School integration started.	An attempt to deal with the increasing demands of blacks for equal rights came in 1964 when President Lyndon Baine Johnson asked for and received the most comprehensive civil-rights act to date; the act specifically prohibited discrimination in voting, education, and the use of public facilities.
7.	1965. President Lyndon B. Johnson signs the Voting Rights Bill.	The Voting Rights Bill, which authorized the suspension of literacy tests.
8.	1967. Thurgood Marshall becomes the first black member of the U.S. Supreme Court.	Historical moment: Thurgood Marshall becomes the first black member of the U.S. Supreme Court.
9.	1983. President Ronald Reagan signs a bill designating the third Monday in January of each year as a federal holiday in honor of Dr. Martin Luther King, Jr.	Millions celebrated the first holiday on January 20, 1986.
10.	2008. The election of Barack Obama, 44th President of the United States	Barack Obama became the first African-American President of the United States.

Furthermore, there can be more victories and progress for African-Americans with unity among one another. However, it will require planning with the intent to execute the plan. The plan has to be a Kingdom Plan if we want the blessings of God. Table 26, Kingdom Man Game Plan, addresses personal, family, church, and community recommendations for men to step-up their game as leaders of their families and households.

TABLE 26 KINGDOM MAN GAME PLAN[134]

No.	Personal Life	Family Life	Church Life	Community Life
1.	Intentionally setting aside time to meet with God daily in His Word and through prayer for the purpose of cultivating spiritual intimacy, drawing down heavenly authority and receiving divine correction and instruction.	Using the dinner table regularly for fellowship, discipleship, addressing the needs within the household, family devotions, and prayer.	Leading my family in weekly or bi-weekly church attendance as well as reviewing with them throughout the week what has been taught.	Regularly sharing the gospel of Jesus Christ throughout my daily life.

---

[134]Tony Evans. *Kingdom Man*. (Carol Stream, Illinois: Tyndale House Publishers, Inc.; 2012), 213.

No.	Personal Life	Family Life	Church Life	Community Life
2.	Seeking to maintain optimal health and to maximize my mental and physical energy through regular exercise, eating a healthy diet, and getting an annual physical exam.	Regularly initiating and planning dates with my wife as well as daily communicating words of affirmation, and routinely setting aside time for in-depth communication.	Regularly meeting with an accountability partner or partners in person and / or by phone for encouragement and authentic relationship.	Joining with other men to arrange and participate in an event designed to reach and influence men in my city.
3.	Carrying out fiscal responsibility in providing for my family, living within my means, paying down any existing debt, giving, and saving for the future.	Developing with my wife an annual family budget that is reviewed together on a monthly basis and developing with her a long-term financial plan that includes maintaining an updated will.	Actively serving in a ministry that maximizes the use of my skills and gifts to help others.	Developing or participating in my church's community outreach ministry such as the National Church Adopt a School Initiative model program.

Consequently, we will never live a victorious life in this world and see all of the promises of God until we come to the knowledge and realization that Christ has done it all. We are waiting for Jesus to finish the work that is already finished. He is finished. On the other hand, we expect Jesus to exceed our expectations, but we fail daily to meet His expectations, even with the help that the Holy Spirit provides for us.

Look at what Jesus has done for us, documented in Hebrews.

Hebrews 10:7-18
Then said I, Lo, I come (in the volume of the book it is written of me,) to do thy will, O God. [8] Above when he said, Sacrifice and offering and burnt offerings and offering for sin thou wouldest not, neither hadst pleasure therein; which are offered by the law; [9] Then said he, Lo, I come to do thy will, O God. He taketh away the first, that he may establish the second. [10] By the which will we are sanctified through the offering of the body of Jesus Christ once for all. [11] And every priest standeth daily ministering and offering oftentimes the same sacrifices, which can never take away sins: [12] But this man, after he had offered one sacrifice for sins for ever, sat down on the right hand of God; [13] From henceforth expecting till his enemies be made his footstool. [14] For by one offering he hath perfected for ever them that are sanctified. [15] Whereof the Holy Ghost also is a witness to us: for after that he had said before, [16] This is the covenant that I will make with them after those days, saith the Lord, I will put my laws into their hearts, and in their minds will I write them; [17] And their sins and iniquities will I remember no more. [18] Now where remission of these is, there is no more offering for sin.

On one hand, we are confessing that we serve a God that can do anything but fail. However, out of our mouths, we are speaking the opposite with our words. I know this is a common occurrence in the African-American churches, regardless of the preaching of Proverbs 18:21, "Death and life are in the power of the tongue: and they that love it shall eat the fruit thereof." For reasons unknown to me, when it matters the most we seem to forget our privileges and power in Christ. When we become aware of our privileges and power, Satan is completely defeated, and his works are destroyed. The enemy wants us to live a defeated and fearful life. We should be aware and conscious of what we confess and confess our position of dominion in Christ. Stop confessing sickness while praying to be healed. Stop confessing being broke and poor while praying for prosperity. Stop confessing loneliness while praying for a companion. Stop confessing difficulties in finding a job while praying for one. Stop confessing defeat while looking for victory. Victory will only manifest itself when we speak the Word of God in faith.

Words have the power to motivate or destroy, energize or deflate, uplift or knock down, build up or tear down, inspire or depress. We can use our words to forgive people that hurt us and extend mercy to them. We can also use our words to inspire and challenge others to greatness. We can start today with a small compliment and words of appreciation to those who least expect it.

Some things in life are ours, but we have to fight to get them; then, we have to fight to keep them. The good news is we have an unfair advantage; it is a fight that we should never lose because the battle has already been won. That means the fight has been fixed, and there is no reason for us to get discouraged or give up. 1 Timothy 6:12, "Fight the good fight of faith, lay hold on eternal life, whereunto thou art also called, and hast professed a good profession before many witnesses."

2 Timothy 4:7, "I have fought a good fight, I have finished my course, I have kept the faith."

The word *fight* in the Greek refers to any competitive contest. Since the word *fight* means a competitive contest, we can safely conclude that "the good fight of faith" is not against Satan. Because we can never have any competitive contest with a liar; and Satan is the father of lies. So, if "the good fight of faith" is not against Satan, then who is it against? It is not against any race, nor is it against a man. It is against our flesh and senses. Our senses do not help us; they hinder us.

The devil does not care and is not concerned about what we believe. Satan can care less about what we hear, see, or feel. The enemy knows our senses keep us where he wants us, stuck in the natural realm, operating under the physical laws of this world with dependence on our senses.

The devil only receives an alert notice when we do something with what we have heard. Translation: "He is put on alert when we finish what we started." If we are hearing the Word of God, we have faith, because the Word of God says, "faith comes by hearing, hearing the Word of God." Therefore, we cannot use lack of faith as an excuse for not doing the will of God. We cannot use the devil as an excuse, because there is nothing competitive about any contest when someone has an unfair advantage. We as Christians have an unfair advantage as long as we believe the Word, live by the Word, and walk by faith. Everything we need has already been appropriated for us. It is now up to us to enter into the spiritual realm of believing and receiving to get what is ours.

I heard one my theology instructors, Bishop Doggett say, "Prophets have prophesied our beginnings and prophesied our endings; but no prophet prophesied about our transition;" and that is the area where we are struggling. We are struggling with the transition phase of our life. No prophet has given us a prophesy about our transition because it takes the good fight of faith to make it through this transition phase.

Yes, during the transition phase we are going to lose things. We are going to feel abandoned, defeated, lost, and forgotten. Nevertheless, if we keep our eyes on Jesus and take them off our problems and battles, we can make it to the other side.

Hope is not enough for us to make it. Hope will keep us going. Hope will keep a smile on our faces and joy in our hearts as we go through. However, hope is not going to stop the bill collectors. Hope is not going to stop the repossession man. Hope is not going to change our situation. I know Jessie Jackson says, "Keep hope alive." Nevertheless, it takes an act of faith to change our situation. Faith without works is dead. We have to mix action with faith to see God move in our situation.

Yes, we are going to go through things we have never experienced before, and there is no one available to bail us out except God. The good news is God is preparing us for an opportunity. When we exercise our faith, and our preparation meets opportunity, we will have success.

God may be silent, but in His silence He does incredible planning and work. Four hundred years passed between Malachi and Matthew without God saying a word, but look what He did. He prepared His only begotten Son to come from heaven down to earth to save sinners like us. After His 400 years of silence, we were blessed with His birth, death, and resurrection. If He is silent now, He is up to something.

The longer we continue in our sins and disobedience, the longer we war against God. Our worldliness keeps us in sin. Everything connected to the flesh must be broken if we want to deal with the real war. The real war is in our hearts, not with the world and not with Satan. There is a price to pay to finish this race. Eventually, we have to be prepared to sacrifice everything that we have for Christ. When and if we do, we can begin to experience restoration and healing in our homes, families, churches, communities, and race as we welcome Christ back into our families.

15. BIBLIOGRAPHY

Berry, Bertice. The Ties That Bind. New York: The Doubleday Publishing Group; 2009.

Corneau, Guy. *Absent Fathers, Lost Sons. The Search for Masculine Identity*. Boston,

Massachusetts: Shambhala Publications, Inc; 1991.

Doe, Mimi and Marsha Walch. *10 Principles for Spiritual Parenting*. New York, NY:

Harper Collins Publishers, Inc.; 1998.

Dyer, Wayne W. *There's a Spiritual Solution to Every Problem*. New York, NY: Harper Collins Publishers; 2001.

Eckhardt, John. *Prayers that Bring Healing*. Lake Mary, Florida: Charisma House; 2010.

Evans, Tony. *Kingdom Man*. Carol Stream, Illinois: Tyndale House Publishers, Inc.; 2012.

Evans, Tony and Chrystal Evans Hurst. *Kingdom Woman*. Carol Stream, Illinois: Tyndale House Publishers, Inc.; 2013.

Farrar, Steve. Point Man. *How A Man Can Lead His Family*. Frisco, Texas: Multnomah Books; 2003.

Hill, Os. TGIF, Today God is First.

Hopkins, Dwight N. *Black Faith and Public Talk*. Maryknoll, New York: Orbis Books; 1999.

Jones J, Mosher WD. Fathers' involvement with their children: United States, 2006–2010. National health statistics reports; no 71. Hyattsville, MD: National Center for Health Statistics. 2013.

Lamb, M. E. (1997). The role of fathers in child development (3rd ed., pp. 49-65, 318-325). New York, NY: John Wiley & Sons; Lamb, M. E.

Ledwidge, Asher. *Saving the Black Culture A Revolution of Hope-Black Unity-Brotherly*

Love. Clermont, Florida: Self-published Asher Ledwidge; 2004.

Ledwidge, Asher. *For The Black Man Soul And Redemption Promoting Black Manhood. Guide to Maintaining a Delicate Balance between Material Consumption and Spiritual Fulfillment*. Clermont, Florida: Nuf-Love Publications; 2001.

Mosley, J., & Thompson, E. (1995). Fathering behavior and child outcomes: (pp. 148-165). Thousand Oaks, CA: Sage.

Popenoe, D. (1996). Life without father: Compelling new evidence that fatherhood and marriage are indispensable for the good of children and society (p. 163). New York, NY: The Free Press; Stanton, G. T. (2003).

Taylor, Kristin Clark. Black Fathers A Call For Healing. (New York, New York: Doubleday; 2003), 36.

Verreen, Winfred Dr. Bible Study Class. Orlando, Florida: Elim Baptist Ministries; 2014.

Internet Resources

Parker, Wayne. Statistics on Fatherless Children in America.

http://fatherhood.about.com/od/fathersrights/a/fatherless_children.htm

Steep, Gina. *Are Men Anti-Church*. Retrieved March 5, 2011 from

http://www.vision.org/visionmedia/article.aspx?id=141

http://americanfreepress.net/?p=14864

http://blackamericaweb.com/2013/02/06/the-history-of-racial-economic-inequality-part-1-slavery/

http://blackfathers.org/2011/09/single-black-fathers-little-known-facts-revealed/

http://blackdemographics.com/culture/religion/

http://www.cdc.gov/nchs/data/nhsr/nhsr064.pdf

http://www.city-data.com/forum/politics-other-controversies/1593583-absent-black-father-causes.html

www.crosswalkmail.com/mcdbqscdbwblcpdkltgvzlmzcslpygg-pwnczqqktwwynsts_thbvhzblclph.html

http://en.m.wikipedia.org/wiki/African-American_family_structure

http://everydaylife.globalpost.com/single-parents-4202.html

http://family.jrank.org/pages/59/African-American-Families-Contemporary-Social-

Influences.html#ixzz1GXJ8pf1h

http://fatherhood.hhs.gov/CFSForum/c4.htm.

http://fatherhood.about.com/od/fathersrights/a/fatherless_
children.htm

http://www.fbi.gov/about-us/cjis/ucr/crime-in-the-u.s/2011/
crime-in-the-u.s.-2011/tables/table-43

http://www.godlikeproductions.com/forum1/
message2092547/pg1

http://www.healthychildren.org/English/family-life/family-dy-
namics/types-of-families/Pages/The-Challenges-of-Single-
Parenthood.aspx

http://www.imom.com/mom-life/
encouragement/5-toughest-single-mom-struggles/

http://love-god-love-others.blogspot.com/2012/03/meaning-of-
fallen-from-grace.html

http://nces.ed.gov/pubsearch/pubsinfo.asp?pubid=2001032.

http://www.pewsocialtrends.org/2013/07/02/
the-rise-of-single-fathers/

http://www.realpictv.com/marriage-and-divorce-in-the-afri-
can-american-community.php

http://psychcentral.com/news/2014/05/04/discrimination-con-
tributes-to-mental-health-woes-in-black-teens/69337.html

http://www.s4.brown.edu/us2010/Data/Report/report0727.pdf

http://rare.us/story/
white-on-black-murder-who-really-is-killing-whom/

CPSIA information can be obtained
at www.ICGtesting.com
Printed in the USA
LVOW11s1533021216
515290LV00001B/23/P